THE
TAX
cure

THOMAS BLACK, MD MBA
WITH CONTRIBUTIONS BY
MIKE PINE, CPA MPAc

THE
TAX
cure

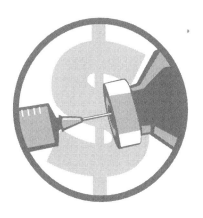

CHANGE THE FACTS OF YOUR
FINANCIAL LIFE TO CREATE
TRUE WEALTH & PEACE OF MIND

Published by Napali Capital

ISBN: 978-1-7379326-0-4

Design by Margaret Cogswell Designs
margaretcogswell.com

To all those in healthcare working nights, weekends, and holidays who sacrafice their own health, family, and happiness. May you find your own freedom. These chaotic times now more than ever have revealed that our prefession takes a toll both physically and mentally.

Find freedom not security.
I wish you the best on your path.

TABLE OF CONTENTS

Part Two
Borrow, Retain, Retire

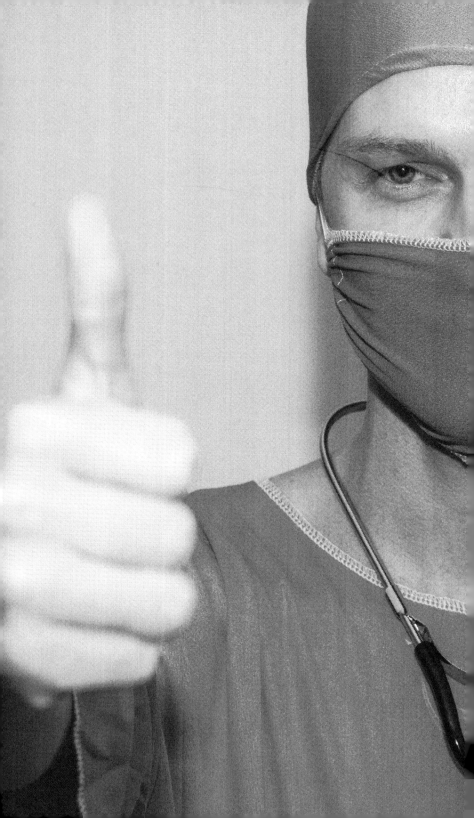

excellence:

Your Way of Life

To build a company, to create jobs, to own a business means you are entitled to legally take full advantage of the United States tax code. I want that for you because I know it will improve your financial security while you continue your medical career and enhance your prospects for retirement.

I also know that the average citizen will not answer the call.

But you are not average. You earned your enrollment in medical school, and following your internship, you earned your first position as a licensed physician. Therefore, developing a lucrative relationship with the tax code is not intimidating. Not for you.

Start by reviewing your personal facts of life. Where are you limiting yourself? What can you change—now— so that your financial life improves?

Occasionally, I'll overhear a conversation where someone is struggling or has suffered a financial loss that ends with a sigh and the comment, "Well, it's only money."

I disagree. Financial well-being is not only money. It is also a matter of mental health, stable relationships with family and friends, and the joy of immersing yourself in a career without worrying about retirement.

I look back and smile when I remember the fear and anxiety I experienced when I purchased my first big assets. There were challenges, to be sure, but my early projects also provided many valuable lessons. Lessons that I quickly put into action so that I could buy more commercial real estate. With my brother, Tim, and some money from investors, I purchased a building for just over $12 million, and two years later sold it for over $21 million.

This is not a boast. This is merely a reminder that I am a doctor too, and it was not long ago that I was being pulled in many directions and was not sure I could be bothered with more tasks, such as buying and managing real estate.

The decision to make changes boils down to a simple question: *Are you willing to accept challenges that have the power to transform you from desperate to blissful?*

In closing, allow me to remind you of what I suspect is the only significant difference between me and you.

I love taxes.

INTRODUCTION
Love Your Taxes

Even while I was attending medical school, I knew that I was going to have a large tax burden once I became a doctor. It pained me when I realized that I would essentially be working free of charge for the Internal Revenue Service for four months of every year with a tax rate of at least 37 percent. In fact, the average doctor pays between 30 and 50 percent of income when combining the various forms of taxation:

- Sales tax
- Payroll tax
- Estate tax
- Property tax
- Income tax

Tax, tax, tax. It was like a slap in the face for a man who had big ideas about becoming a doctor so that he could serve the greater good. *If I was willing to put in the work, why did Uncle Sam have to pick my pocket so excessively?*

Certainly, I wanted to contribute my fair share of federal and state taxes, or at least what I imagined my fair share should be. Yet, every time I did the math, I stumbled on the mental hurdle of imagining myself working in the stressful setting of a hospital emergency room without being paid for what amounted to four months. *Every year. For the rest of my life.*

By the time I began my residency in Indianapolis, I realized I was not the only medical professional concerned about taxes. Veteran doctors often complained about the harm they saw in excess taxation. Their bill was the single greatest payment they made each year. It hurt most in those years when they did not see significant growth in their stock portfolios which was their main investment vehicle.

Working 100 hours a week in the hospital was exhausting, but I was so enthralled with finance that I made time to read about money and wealth creation. My tax bracket was not my only incentive. Living on a resident's salary with my wife, Micaela, and our kids inspired me to seek an alternative path: one that was different from the typical road to retirement paved by so many doctors who had come before me.

The core idea was defined by one word: ownership.

My method for achieving this goal was also quite simple: create assets and cash flow to reduce my tax footprint. This would give me the freedom to choose when, where, and how I would work in medicine.

After I graduated from residency, we relocated to Texas where my family and I began a remarkable new phase of life. But did Micaela and I sell the Indianapolis home we had purchased? No. We decided to keep the property—our first real estate asset— and become landlords. We rented our former home to—guess who? An incoming resident, who would need housing for three years. It was easy to do with a little help from a local realtor who taught me methods for beating down taxes. But there was a downside.

Since I was not living in the home, we could no longer claim the mortgage as a tax deduction: one of our prime reasons for buying the property. Initially, I thought we would miss that perk. After all, my goal was to reduce our tax bill. My mood took an upswing when I learned that my loss would be replaced by something much more powerful.

Obviously, Micaela and I would collect rental income each month from our tenant in Indianapolis. That sum more than covered our mortgage payment, and we felt good about that. And, a new and greater advantage came our way in the form of *depreciation*. Remember that word. In the chapters ahead, I will reveal why this perfectly legal tax tool far outweighs the benefit of a mere mortgage deduction.

In my first book, *The Passive Income Physician*, I defined two kinds of doctors. Dr. Desperate knew nothing about money and taxation and, therefore, traveled a challenging career path. Dr. Bliss, on the other hand, understood that the 5,800-page United

States tax code was his friend and so applied it with skill and enthusiasm to build wealth. Which camp would you prefer to join?

Most of that massive and instructive document invites doctors and every other citizen in America to pay much less tax if they will stimulate the economy. I can hear you groan. You are an exceptionally good physician whose heart is in the right place, and you are pushing back: "I'm too busy being a doctor to stimulate Main Street."

I get it. I have been there. I am on your side.

However, it is time to have a frank conversation about the misconceptions that often thwart a doctor's quest and need for wealth. Let's start with a few real-world facts:

An income that defines you as an upper-class citizen does not necessarily make you wealthy.

Recent legislation forbids business opportunities for doctors, such as partnerships in many hospital ownership structures.

Today, it is harder than ever for a doctor to become rich as a sole proprietor. The family doctor is a quaint icon of the past that has been replaced by corporate medical groups that have shrunk physician salaries.

We cannot demand that the working world of medicine and money change for our benefit, and we do not need to. Change must come from another resource that is malleable, easily identifiable, and generous. It must come from within.

Change the facts of your financial life—the limiting beliefs that handcuff your effort to excel—and you'll begin to experience a new, expansive relationship with money. The change begins when you embrace the tax code.

In these pages, I invite you to shake hands with your new best friend— that scary beast you may believe is much too fat, ugly, and intricate to understand. Nonsense. Believe it or not, the United States tax code is on our side. It wants us to succeed beyond our wildest dreams. And by the end of this book, you will understand why.

Yes, I know you are being pulled in many directions and do not want to be bothered with more tasks. I also know that you would rather be blissful than desperate and inclined to smile not gripe when meeting with the president of your physicians' group. I know all this because I am a doctor too, but with one significant difference.

I love taxes.

MY FATHER:
THE DOCTOR I RARELY SAW
Mike Pine

I grew up in a medical family. My father was a founding partner at Emory University Clinic in Atlanta, GA. My mother was a registered nurse, and even my stepmother had a medical credential: she was a PharmD.

My dad was a pulmonologist specializing in critical care, and when I was growing up, it seemed he was either at work or on-call. As a teaching physician, he worked his tail off while making an impact on thousands of lives. He had an impressive career. Yet, I'll never forget the day he confessed his greatest regret.

"Mike, I wish I had spent more time with you and your sister when you were kids," he said.

But what could he do? Many people beyond our family circle depended on him under life and death circumstances, and he was helping to educate the future physicians of the world.

One of the most stunning moments my sister and I shared was in the twilight of our father's career. After decades of serving others, Emory University honored him by creating a chair in his name donated by an incredibly generous patient that provided a very large grant in sincere appreciation to the impact my father made on his family's lives. We both traveled to Atlanta for the ceremony and were astounded to see the hundreds of people who had gathered to celebrate their mentor and tell stories of Dad's dedication. Younger doctors hailed him as a gifted teacher, and patients thanked him for the profound impact he had on their lives. The stories brought my sister and me to tears. We finally recognized why our father was absent from much of our childhood. We were incredibly proud, and yet ...

Physicians should not have to give up so much of their lives to be fulfilled in their work. It is not fair. That is why my mission as a tax expert is to help medical professionals and others improve their finances by reducing their tax burden.

My dad started his practice before the Stark Law. The regulatory legislation now limits the way doctors can invest. Fortunately, for half of his career, Dad made a decent living. Although even without the Stark restraints, he never attained the financial freedom I think he deserved and though he is now retired, his means are relatively modest.

As a kid, I knew my dad loved me. However, my sister and I will never get back those years when we should have had our father by our side.

My childhood experiences definitely shaped my professional goals.

As a junior at Montana State University, I earned an internship with Price Waterhouse Cooper's (PwC). I began to learn how to prepare tax returns for some of the largest private equity and venture capital funds in Silicon Valley. My four-month internship coincided with tax season. I worked 100-hour weeks and literally fell in love with taxes.

Once I returned to MSU to finish my business bachelor's degree, I could not wait to join the real world so that I could practice all I'd learned about tax forms and strategies. After college graduation, I sat for all four parts of the grueling CPA licensing exam and earned passing grades for each.

Tax preparation was fascinating, and I could not get enough. That is, not until that day I woke up and realized that I was following in my father's footsteps: My job at one of the biggest tax firms in America was eating up my life. Spending 80 hours a week as a cog in an assembly line was unsatisfying. In theory, I was making a real-world impact with billion-dollar funds. However, I had no connection to the actual taxpayers; and therefore, I had no idea whether they were taking advantage of the tax optimization strategies we had prescribed. I thought, "Hey, Mike, I thought you decided to become a CPA so that you could achieve a better work-life balance than your dad!"

To get back on track, I returned to MSU to improve my credentials and earned a Masters of Professional

Accountancy (M.P.Ac.). From there I joined a smaller tax firm in Dallas that focused on developing the best methods for serving clients.

That's my story. What's yours? Perhaps you're an overworked–– and well-paid physician who is tired of being stressed out every tax season. If so, this book was created for you. Let's get started so that you too can enjoy a better balance of work, home-life, and financial security.

IMPORTANT INFORMATION REGARDING CAPITAL GAINS TAX RATES AND TAX LAW CHANGES

Throughout history, the United States has generally recognized that lower tax rates for capital investments helped increase the amount of money that the private sector would invest in businesses. Tax laws have always been changing and will continue to do so.

At the time of the writing of this book, significant tax benefits exist for income that qualifies for long-term capital gains tax treatment. Such gains (generally speaking) are taxed at a flat rate of 20 percent.

Additionally, any passive investment gains are taxed an additional 3.8 percent, making most passive long-term capital gains taxed at a total rate of 23.8%.

In May of 2021, the U.S. Treasury Department released its *Green Book*. This book outlines what the Administration is currently asking Congress to enact with tax legislation. If enacted into law, some of the requests would increase long-term capital gains tax rates as high as 43.4 percent for taxpayers that earn over a set threshold. $1,000,000 is the requested threshold amount. This threshold is defined by the taxpayer's Adjusted Gross Income (AGI). The fact that the threshold would be based on AGI is an extremely important point for the readers of this book.

AGI is not an absolute for anyone that proactively plans and optimizes their taxes. AGI can be increased and decreased by the actions that a taxpayer takes. This book's fundamental concept attempts to illustrate that *taxpayers can and should control their taxes and their AGI.*

If such new laws are, indeed, enacted, it would be that much more critical for you to proactively plan and utilize the tax code as a map to enhance and optimize the growth of your wealth. ~~Managing your AGI to be under $1,000,000 in tax yea~~rs that you anticipate long-term capital gains is very doable for a large majority of taxpayers.

The Green Book maintains preferential tax treatment for long-term capital gains for income under the threshold. It is also vital to note that historically speaking, the actual tax laws that Congress has passed generally were quite different than what the *Green Book* requested.

It is also very likely that a new Congress will return the incentive for the private sector to make capital investments in the near future. Therefore, we think that the planning strategies that include utilizing the benefits of preferential capital gains tax rates remain essential.

PART 1
Depreciation Nation

chapter 1

Antacid for Tax Anxiety

As tax time approaches many physicians begin to feel a little sick in the stomach or even depressed. It is an annual and sometimes grueling ritual that reminds these dedicated men and women that a generous income does not guarantee wealth, despite the impression in America that all doctors are rich. Gastritis is usually accompanied by worrisome questions:

How much is the Internal Revenue Service (IRS) going to take this year?

How hard must I work before my finances are no longer so fragile?

How do I get ahead when I am already working 60-80 hours a week?

Thankfully, there is a remedy for these symptoms that many physicians can access with a simple mind shift. It begins by accepting that taxes are not the problem. Let's stop thinking of them as the enemy.

It is futile to think of taxes as flesh-eating bacteria that well-paid professionals must battle throughout their careers. In fact, the tax code is good medicine when it is properly understood and embraced. It provides incentives and instructions for how to reduce your burden and make the best use of your money— even when you are carrying debt.

I was once a member of the Anti-Tax Club, who could barely suppress a sneeze or the tremors as April approached. Why the change of heart?

I began to make this turnaround upon examining how most of us initially learned about taxes––usually from a parent or comedian who portrayed taxes as the kissing cousin of mortality: both are inevitable. Not true. Taxation will likely always be around, but it is not intended to be ruinous.

To unlock the magical realm of taxation, we must acknowledge that taxes, as we know them today, were not born in 1776 when America came to be. Initially, only the wealthy were taxed for obvious reasons: everyone assumed they had plenty of money and could afford to share. Then World War II came along, and our government realized that taxing people of other income levels was a great way to raise revenue to do battle and restore what had been devastated by war.

Obviously, our nation's tax code has been revised and amended through the years by White House administrations and Congress. Even so, most physicians and other citizens continue to believe that our tax code was and is intended to raise money. Some might call it robbery by Uncle Sam who lines his coffers with our hard-earned wages. This is incorrect.

This misperception can be erased by examining the 5800-pages of our nation's tax code? But do you really want to? Probably not. Nevertheless, if you want to know every damn thing about lowering your taxes, However, I know a secret: you will only need to peruse about 30 pages.

But wait! Haven't we been raised to believe that the government wants our money?

Cash is nice, to be sure, but even better is enterprise. That is why more than 99.4 percent of our tax code is written to stimulate economic activity in areas such as agriculture, science, education, and energy. These businesses will increase the income that can be taxed to some degree; but more importantly, each new entity will create jobs and, my favorite area of interest, housing. In other words, the United States tax code encourages us to be brave and inventive and it gives us ample incentive to thrive by defining legal tax reductions.

Any physician looking for a sure-fire cure for taxation blues needs to look no further than the laws on the books that allow us to create as much wealth as we wish, while also decreasing our tax burden.

My Valentine to taxes began when I changed the facts of my financial life and finally understood that wealth is not a matter of how much money you make, but rather how much income you keep.

Well, in truth, it is not quite that simple. *You must be wise in the ways you invest your saved income.*

Tax Concept/Risk-Reward
MIKE PINE

Entrepreneurial risk is what it all comes down to. Not every investment makes money. Many lose money. Physicians must always consider risk versus reward.

Yet the opportunities for growing the economy for the well-being of the public are endless. And it is only fair to receive an economic reward if you took the risk.

Congress recognizes that investments stimulate economic growth and, therefore, provide jobs that ultimately create more taxes. That is why you are rewarded with some tax advantages.

chapter 2

Where the Money Grows

The tax code was written for the wealthy. Have a problem with that? Possibly you do, because it is hard to feel wealthy while overworked and paying down an enormous student debt and a mortgage and saving for your children's college educations. That said, the phrase "fake it until you make it" may be appropriate here.

Make financial decisions as though you are a member of the wealthy class. See the bigger picture. The shift from tax-hater to tax-lover will not immediately change your finances but it will open your mind to significant new possibilities.

In a very real sense, the incentives are a road map paved by our government so that health professionals and others fully understand how to begin creating expansive wealth. Now that the doctor is not hating taxes, the question becomes how can he or she get involved in new ventures without discarding the love of caring for patients? Follow the road map, of course.

Shift your priorities so that you put more time, money, and talents into activities that grow the economy by producing jobs and housing. In many ways, utilizing the tax code to the fullest to save as much money in taxes as possible is not only smart, but it may be among the most patriotic things you can do.

Unfortunately, even though the tax law concepts are not difficult to understand, some busy doctors too often hold onto negative and limiting opinions about taxes and, therefore, merely pass along their receipts and income data to their tax advisor. How many times have you or your colleagues said, "I let my CPA handle my taxes"? The truth is your advisor can only *prepare* your returns. That prep will include advice about your particular situation, and perhaps even explain rules that may help reduce your taxes. But the advisor cannot take real, profoundly effective steps to reduce your taxes. Only *you* can do that. And it will not eat up hours of your day to grasp the concepts that are most productive.

After all, the tax code—the road map—is a treasure map. Why would you not want to follow this map when there is ample proof that it eventually leads to expansive wealth? Your taxes will decrease, while your profits and investment returns rise. You will create the freedom you want and the practice you envisioned free of financial restriction. Imagine practicing because you have a passion for medicine rather than a means to the future.

Years ago, when I was still a resident, I began asking myself some serious questions with the hope the answers would take me down a very lucrative road.

> How do I leverage my profession given the restrictions in government laws that preclude advantages of healthcare ownership?

> Where is the new leverage in the changing landscape?

The answer for me was real estate. In the early going, I was, like many other real estate investors, focused on the cash flow. That was fine at first, but it was only the beginning.

Fortunately, I continued to learn and slowly broadened my knowledge. The discoveries I made brought even greater benefits, some of which are commonly overlooked or misunderstood. Still, my personal breakthroughs would not have occurred if I had not changed the "facts," those limiting financial beliefs that had shaped me.

The facts we embrace can be limiting. When I hear someone begin a comment with, "I know for a fact ..." I often cringe. I've come to believe that what we know for certain may actually be a blind spot. We become fixated on our 100 percent grasp of a fact that is blocking our ability to broaden our view and see something larger and more complete.

This is certainly true of the many doctors who know for a fact that their annual tax obligation will be painful. Let's change that fact of life.

INFORMED FACTS OF LIFE

In my youth, my decisions were based on the facts of life as I understood them. But how well was I interpreting information? I had some big blind spots, but don't we all? During my service in the U.S. Navy, my understanding of "facts" began to grow. No, I could not change basic facts such as the sun rises in the east and sets in the west, but I could deepen my appreciation for the processes of the world and, in response, make better decisions.

That's what I mean by changing the facts of your tax life: *become better informed.* As a result, you will make better use of the laws your tax preparer must abide by. The concept of expanding your worldview may seem vague and unwieldy. That's why I focus on the "facts" and urge you to group the guiding facts of your life into three categories: business, investment, and personal pursuits.

BUSINESS: This area of your life is likely driven by your medical education and not actual business training. Although the concept of the small-town doctor is largely a thing of the past, even when accepting a job at a large medical facility, you are in business for yourself. Deepen your knowledge of what this means to you. How is it helping or limiting your financial life?

INVESTMENT: Many doctors hope the stock market via mutual funds will help them build wealth if they are disciplined about contributing each year. The fact is, you may be guided by money market generalities that are not helping you achieve your goals. Deconstruct the facts that are shaping your investment decisions.

PERSONAL PURSUITS: This is an area many doctors may overlook when considering taxes and improving their financial portfolios. Our personal lives often reveal our true interests, which when reviewed, may shine a light on a topic, hobby, or curiosity that could reshape your facts of life. For example, despite the impossible demands of residency, I carved out some time to read about finance and real estate. Why? I really loved the topic. I am now the co-founder of a thriving asset management firm—a fact I never could have imagined when I began reading about property.

Tax Concept/
Long-Term Capital Gains
MIKE PINE

Only a small portion of the Internal Revenue Code involves the assessment and levying of taxes. A supermajority of it provides enticement to make investments that are expected to support the nation. The government entices our society by providing tax breaks for those who make investments in chosen areas of commerce and industries. By receiving a material tax reduction in gains on any investment, the rate of return on investment is inherently and considerably higher.

Consider a $100,000 investment that doubles to $200,000. If the gain of 100K were to be taxed at the current highest marginal tax rate of 37 percent, the investor would have after-tax earnings of $63,000 (or a real 63 percent cash return after-tax). If that investor could get long-term capital gains tax treatment for the same investment, and by materially participating in the investment, they would avoid the net investment income tax. They would only pay 20 percent and be left with a gain of $80,000. *Be sure to review the important information on page 24 about possible changes in the capital gains tax rates.*

That's an 80 percent return versus a 63 percent return, or an increase of 27 percent on the return. Real money.

chapter 3

Your Money Is Not the Government's Money

The desperate doctor lives under a cloud of misinformation: Uncle Sam owns my money. Not true.

Unless you live in North Korea, the money you earn and the wealth that you build belong to you. You may be required to give some of it to the government to help build roads, maintain the military, and sustain schools. But, at its core, you worked for it, and it is *your* money.

Once my knowledge about taxation began to grow, I interviewed CPAs and preparers in search of someone who could help me achieve my goals. The experience was frustrating because after reading about tax laws and various strategies, I wanted a tax expert who would embrace my ideas and plan for the future—*my future.*

I admit I tended to be the squeaky wheel. I would go into the meetings with a long list of questions. "Well, what about this? What about that?" In fairness, I am sure I wore down some of the people I interviewed. One advisor grew frustrated with my ideas and questions because they illuminated his ignorance. He did not want to admit what he did not understand.

In other interviews, the advisor would default with, "Well, this is the way I do it," or "That is risky." They could not grasp the perfectly legal ideas I was suggesting. In some meetings, I was not taken seriously, or the preparer did not want to bother with me because I would be a "small" or insignificant client. I was not low-hanging fruit. At the time, I was a couple of years out of residency and earning about $300,000 annually and paying a boatload of quarterly taxes.

As you can tell, a cookie-cutter approach to hiring an advisor will not work. I refused to settle on just any CPA, and I suggest you adopt the same attitude. If you're speaking with someone who cannot embrace your goals and perspective, why would you want them to do your taxes?

Once you grasp the true purpose of the tax code, you will begin to trust that you have the right to reduce your taxes at every turn. You are not being sneaky or seeking tricky loopholes. You are merely following tax rules that will become easy to understand. Once you accept this fact of life, you quickly become Dr. Bliss and harvest more value for yourself.

TAX PLANNING IS A MUST

Too many doctors ignore taxes when investing and planning their wealth strategy. They neglect to consider how their potential profit will impact their tax obligations. This is just one more characteristic of Dr. Desperate.

Since taxes are your biggest annual expense, you need information that clarifies your end result before you invest. This practice may reveal that you are making less on your favorite investments than you initially thought. Conversely, you may discover that investments you ignored or shied away from promise a better tax outcome.

Prior to my financial awakening, I did not understand how to evaluate various investment vehicles to fully grasp their tax consequences. When I compared real estate to other investments before taxes and without debt, everything looked relatively the same. The first duplex I bought as a rental property after my residency is a perfect example.

The property was purchased for $500,000, with a $100,000 down payment and a loan of $400,000. Suppose the annual return on your investment of $100,000 is 6 percent. Then suppose you make another investment in a mutual fund with an 8 percent return. Is this second investment better than the first because the percentage of return is higher? Let's compare.

The 8 percent return from the mutual fund will get you $8,000 before taxes. But you will pay capital gains tax of about 20 percent (the current rate as of the writing of this book), counting both federal and state taxes, leaving you with an after-tax return of $6,400.

By comparison, the lowly 6 percent return on the real estate investment will get you a before-tax return of $6,000. That doesn't sound so good, does it? Think again. You won't pay any tax on $6,000. Thanks to the magic of depreciation, that gain from real estate is less than your after-tax return of $6,400 in the stock market. Or so it seems.

But we are not finished.

There are more advantages included in your real estate investment. In addition to the tax-free cash flow—$6,000—it also provides $27,000 in depreciation of your rental property. Remember, I was not living in that duplex, I was the landlord. Let's continue.

Since there is a positive cash flow of $6,000, you subtract that amount from your $27,000 depreciation figure.

$27,000 minus $6,000 = $21,000

The remaining $21,000 of depreciation from a real estate property can now be used to lower taxes on your doctor's salary or whatever other business income you may have if you are able to qualify. Additionally, it can offset income from other investments. As an example, a $300,000 annual salary is reduced to $279,000. In a typical 37 percent tax bracket, that means Dr. Bliss reduces his tax payment by about $7,700.

Now let's go back to the beginning. You have two investment opportunities to consider:

You can put $100,000 into a mutual fund and potentially see a nice after-tax annual return of $6,400.

You can put that same $100,000 into real estate and potentially see $6,000 cash flow and the $7,700 reduction of tax for a return of $13,700! This choice has a greater impact on your goal of reducing taxes and expanding wealth.

By now you can probably guess what choice Dr. Desperate and Dr. Bliss would make. What's your choice?

Tax Concept/ Rate of Return
MIKE PINE

One of the most important concepts in wealth generation is the power of compounding. According to the Rule of 72, a dollar invested with an annual rate of 7.2 percent will double in value every 10 years. Assuming a dollar is invested with an average annual rate of return of 7.2 percent per year, in 30 years one buck would be worth eight bucks.

$1 multiplied by 30 years with a 7.2 percent return = $8

The 7.2 percent with the 27 percent increase mentioned in the previous tax remedy chapter creates an actual annual return of 9.14 percent. That increase would double the value of one buck every 7.9 years. In 30 years, one buck would be worth nearly $14.00.

$1 multiplied by 30 years with an after tax 9.14 percent return = $14.00

That's nearly twice the return on the same dollar in the same kind of economic investment when you avail yourself of the capital gains tax rate. *Again, refer to the information on page 24.*

chapter 4

Entities and Their Strategies

The concept of creating a tax strategy is not as difficult as most people think. Start by deciding what you want to accomplish.

> Do you want to decrease your income taxes?

> Are there state and local or provincial taxes you want to reduce?

> What about property taxes?

> Do you own equipment in your business or real estate that is taxed on its value?

And by the way, if you own a business, you will also want to reduce your sales tax, value-added tax, excise taxes, and payroll taxes. Not to mention, if you plan on leaving anything to your kids you probably want to reduce your estate taxes too.

Each of these taxes requires its own specific strategy to keep them as low as possible. For now, let us focus on income tax since that's the one that probably keeps you and your colleagues up at night. In this example, I will assume you are in the 37 percent or higher tax bracket given rules set by the current administration at the time of writing this book. Many doctors reach this level of taxation when we consider federal income tax and local income taxes. Also, we do not want a reduction just for this tax year. We want the improvement to be permanent.

Most tax plans throughout the world are temporary. Like many people in the United States, you probably have an IRA or 401(k) which gives you a tax deduction each year. The money will be taxed when you withdraw it later in life upon retirement.

The primary reason for this type of tax planning is that you will be in a lower tax bracket when you remove the money than when you deposited it. This is all predicated on the idea that you are planning to retire on less money than you now earn. So, in other words, you are expecting to retire "poor," by reducing the annual income that you earn while practicing medicine. I have always taken issue with this presumption because I do not understand why anyone would want to reduce their standard of living. I certainly do not!

There are a couple of reasons why this type of temporary planning is so prevalent.

First, the reality is you will probably be in an even higher tax bracket if you're going to have access to the same amount of money in retirement as you do while employed. Why? Because you will not have the same deductions, exemptions, or credits you currently enjoy for your children, for your house, or even for your business. After all, you want to be retired.

Second, temporary tax planning is popular because it is so easy, particularly for tax planners. For example, in a tax-deferred savings plan, you basically lose control of your money. Not just here in the United States, but in nations throughout the world that restrict when you can withdraw your own hard-earned money. That concept does not take much planning or thinking. It is what it is.

Permanent tax planning takes more thought and skill, but it means that the tax savings we plan for we can keep. *We never have to give them back to Uncle Sam.*

Using the permanent tax-savings techniques available to entrepreneurs and investors allows you to avoid the pitfalls of temporary or deferral techniques. Instead of increasing your tax rates, you increase your control over your wealth. Rather than increasing your risk in the stock market, you reduce your risk by investing in hard assets. And by maintaining control over your wealth, you may increase your returns.

Change the facts of your life. Think long term when planning your road map to lower taxes and greater wealth.

THINKING THROUGH YOUR TAX STRATEGY

Start with the facts and nothing but the facts. Where are you now financially? Next, imagine where you want to be further down the road, in the future. It is the same as planning a trip: You know your starting point and where you intend to travel. Being specific about the future—regardless of where you are now—will have a major impact on your road map. A few questions you should ask:

> What investments do I have now?

> What business entities (e.g., corporations and partnerships) do I own now?

> What are my plans for my business and investments?

How sure am I that tax returns are being prepared in the best way possible?

How often do I hear from my tax advisor? (You should hear a minimum of four times a year from your tax advisor.)

How old are my children?

Do I plan to have more children?

Are my children interested in working in my business (or do I want them to be if they are too young right now)?

How secure is my job?

Do I need to set aside money to help my parents in their old age?

These questions will likely lead to more questions about your specific situation. That is fine. Once you have a specific picture of where you want to go, you can start forming your strategy. But remember two things: You want it to be flexible as you look at the big picture. By flexible, I mean you want your strategy to allow for changes in your life. The only thing we really know for sure is that life tomorrow will be different than life today. You may have more children tomorrow, your business might change, and even your marital status can change. Be sure your tax strategy is built with these possible changes in mind. As for the big picture, avoid choices that give you big tax savings now only to cause bigger problems later for you in your business or family life.

PICKING ENTITIES

When working with a doctor to create their tax strategy, I like to begin with the business entities. The right entity can help reduce your taxes almost immediately.

Remember, an entity is just a form of ownership, such as a corporation or a limited liability company. Each nation throughout the world has its own best entities for different purposes. Let's look at the different types of entities and some general rules for when to use them.

There are four primary entity types: trusts, partnerships, corporations, and limited liability companies. Most countries have some form of each of these entities, though they may have different names.

TRUSTS

Trusts are universal throughout the world. Three primary people are involved in a trust. First is the settlor or grantor. This is the person who forms the trust and puts the assets into the trust. The second is the trustee. This is the person or company in charge of taking care of the trust. The third person is the beneficiary. This is the person who will reap the rewards of the trust assets. Any trust can have one or multiple grantors, trustees, and beneficiaries.

Trusts are used for a variety of purposes but primarily to transfer assets from one person to another. They are particularly useful in family planning where parents or grandparents want to transfer assets to their children or grandchildren. They can also be used in transferring assets to charities and other organizations. They are essential for creating solid estate planning. It was not until I had a significant amount of assets that I finally understood the need for a trust. Trusts can be great devices for tax planning and for creating a legal barrier for the protection of your holdings. When you consider the liability we have as doctors, this is an absolute must once you break out of your routine facts of life.

PARTNERSHIPS

Partnerships are perhaps the most flexible of the various entities. A partnership exists whenever two or more individuals or entities own and operate a business or investment together and have not decided to use another type of entity, such as a corporation. The income and loss from partnerships is reported in the tax returns of each partner, instead of paying tax in the partnership. There are two varieties of partnerships: general partnerships and limited partnerships.

General partnerships allow every partner to make decisions for the partnership. And all partners are typically responsible for the debts of the partnerships. So, you can imagine that general partnerships can be a little dangerous if there is a chance the partnership might get sued at some time in the future.

Limited partnerships include at least one general partner and one limited partner. A limited partner is limited to investing and has no say in the daily operations of the partnership. They do not have any personal responsibility for partnership debts beyond the amount they invested. Additionally, in the United States, the income received by limited partners usually is classified as passive income. Limited partnerships are good to use when one person oversees the business and the others are passive investors.

CORPORATIONS

Corporations are the entities most recognized around the world for owning and operating businesses. In the United States, currently, there are lower tax rates for small businesses, special benefits when a small business loses money or goes out of business, and there is even a special class of small businesses called an S corporation that allows the owners to report the business income on their personal tax return.

Have a business partner? Form your own entity taxed as an S corporation and have that entity be the partner in your business rather than you personally. This structure will reduce your self-employment taxes and provide maximum flexibility to you and your partner. S corporations for doctors that are independent contractors receiving a 1099 from their contracted parties are particularly useful in this regard. An S corporation will allow you to treat your services as a company and can reduce payroll taxation, thereby reducing your overall taxation through the entity rather than paying payroll taxes on every dollar earned.

Corporations are particularly useful if you plan to become a public company, that is a company that is owned by lots of people. They are also good for protecting your personal assets from lawsuits, as we will see in another chapter.

LIMITED LIABILITY COMPANIES

Limited liability companies exist so that you can have the asset protection that you would normally get as a limited partner while still having a say in the company. Remember, limited partners cannot control the company. Members of the LLC, though, can have full management control without being fully liable. For this reason, many businesses in the United State are now formed as an LLC instead of a partnership.

Each of these entities has a place in your tax strategy. For example, you may want to use an LLC to own your real estate investment properties, a corporation (or LLC taxed as a corporation) to own the assets you want to transfer to your children. You likely will want to use trusts to protect assets you set aside for your children from creditors and others, particularly while they are young.

YOUR ENTITY TEAM

You will need an attorney involved in this process along with your tax advisor. Entities are the foundation for your tax strategy. Once you have your entities in place, you can begin to take full advantage of all the tax benefits we have, and will discuss, to permanently reduce your income, estate, and other taxes now and for generations to come.

In summary, you begin *here and now* by defining the facts of your financial life. Then describe in detail your future. Include flexibility in your plan so that you are prepared for unforeseen changes. Always assess the big picture.

Once you have your strategy in place you need to implement it. This means living it every day of your life. This is how the facts of life change in meaningful ways.

The more you use your strategy, the more comfortable you will become with it. Remember that you can lower your taxes every day just by putting your tax strategy into action.

LLCs AND TAXATION

Your limited liability company (LLC) can be whatever you want it to be. The LLC has become the entity of choice for United States asset protection purposes. But what about for tax purposes?

The good news is your LLC can be whatever it wants to be—a sole proprietorship, a partnership, a C corporation, or an S corporation. This flexibility gives you the best of the tax and asset protection worlds. The key here is that you can have the best of both worlds when it comes to the tax law. Simply by understanding that LLCs can be treated any way you want for tax purposes, you have asset protection and still get the tax advantages of the S corporation, C corporation, or partnership rules. (By the way, Dr. Desperate never took the time to learn this.)

Once you decide which type of entity you want for tax purposes, be sure you make the proper entity tax election by checking the correct box on the IRS entity election form. If you do not make the election, the IRS will choose for you which tax entity you will be: a sole proprietorship for single-member LLCs or a partnership for multi-member LLCs. In some cases, you can make your entity election at any time during the year. This election gives you great flexibility in your tax planning. The benefits of this combined entity structure are huge. Because you own the business as a partnership, you can distribute income differently than you allocate income. There is a lot of flexibility when you have a clear understanding of the different entity types and your tax advisor has a clear understanding of your goals and circumstances.

MAXIMIZING THE 20 PERCENT PASS-THROUGH DEDUCTION

The United States has a special deduction equal to the lesser of 20 percent of business net income or 50 percent of wages from a business. Not all payments to a partner qualify as wages for this purpose. So, if the two business owners in the strategy above formed a partnership and had no employees, they might not receive the 20 percent deduction if their income is over a certain level. And they would pay high social security taxes on all their partnership income.

However, if they own their partnerships through their S Corporations, not only would they severely reduce their social security taxes, they will also create W-2 income that would allow them to take the 20 percent deduction.

Tax Concept/
Surfing Tax Brackets
MIKE PINE

Capital gains tax rates are only one of many concepts that may cure your tax anxiety. *See the note on page 24 for important information on possible changes.* When combined with the low-hanging fruit of depreciation—especially when you use the legally available concept of accelerated depreciation—you can achieve after-tax returns of even a larger increase over time. And it does not need to take 30 years.

Our nation uses a "progressive" tax system, which means the higher your income the more you'll be taxed. This fact of life provides some great opportunities to increase your after-tax returns over time by surfing tax brackets.
The surfing concept maximizes your tax returns in two steps:

1. Strategically plan in what year you recognize income

2. Choose the year you wish to take the available tax deductions

This provides yet another multiplier effect for exponentially growing your personal wealth.

chapter 5

Lower Taxes Creates Self-Perpetuating Money

As a doctor right out of training, I will never forget my first month's compensation. Oh boy! After all those years of deferred fun and gratification, I was ready to let the good times roll. As an independent contractor in an emergency medicine group everything was amazing and going my way—until the following April.

I was astonished when I looked at my tax bill. Even though I had been educating myself for years in preparation for this moment, and I had dutifully made quarterly tax payments, it had not been enough. I came up drastically short.

Deflated and disappointed in my application of the tax code as I understood it, I heard myself repeat a mantra that may be familiar to you: "Deductions.

Deductions. I need more deductions to reduce my taxes!"

When you set up your tax strategy correctly, you can immediately reduce how much money comes out of your paycheck. Or, if you are an entrepreneur or investor, you can reduce your quarterly tax payment. You do not have to wait until tax time to enjoy the benefit of lower taxes.

I eventually learned that in many cases we can file amended tax returns at any time, which will correct errors or returns for the previous year. In some cases, you can even carry back losses from the current year to a prior year, use the loss to offset the prior year's income, and get a refund in the here and now.

This part of the tax code was made apparent in March 2020 when the federal government passed the Coronavirus Aid, Relief, and Economic Security (CARES) Act. The amendment allowed for net operating losses to be carried back five years. This means that if you paid tax in the past five years, your 2020 losses could be reduced so that you qualify for a refund. This change in the law was helpful to me as well as my investor partners. We received several hundreds of thousands of dollars in tax refunds! Where did this money then go? It was invested back into our assets portfolio to improve our future cash flow and deductions, just as I described in Chapter 2. The CARES Act is more proof that the tax code is intended to be your friend.

Most doctors do not realize they can begin to reduce their taxes right now. Everybody can and should, every day of the week. *Remember our motto: To change your taxes you must change your facts.* All it takes is learning the difference between bad, good, and better income, and then learning how to turn your expenses into tax deductions. The cool part is that every expense has the potential to reduce your taxes. I am serious, *every* expense.

I know I am repeating myself, but this truth must become self-evident: **You, and only you, have the power and the control over your money and your taxes.** Nobody else. This includes your tax preparer and your tax advisor. They cannot reduce your taxes. They can only help equip you to do so. Year-end tax planning is important but year-round tax planning is better. Make a promise to reduce your taxes every day of the week. I will show you how.

SIMPLE CHANGES: DEDUCT YOUR MEALS

Eat while you work and save taxes. Business meals are a great way to spend time with employees, clients, and customers. You can discuss business and turn your meal expense into a deductible expense. The desperate doctor usually brings a frozen dinner to work, pops it into the microwave, and eats alone.

Almost any expense can be deductible in the right circumstance, including food, cars, travel, and even your house—if you change your facts so that the expense is a business one.

What is a business expense? In the United States, the tax law requires each business deduction to meet three tests.

First, the expense must have a business purpose, which means the primary purpose. To be deductible, the purpose of a meal must be business. This means you must have a conservation about business with your dining partner before, during, or after the meal. Another valid deduction is a business meal that occurs when you are traveling for business.

Second, the expense must be ordinary. An expense is ordinary if it is "customary and usual." This means that within your industry, the expense should be typical of what would be spent, both in the amount of the expense and how often a person in your position would have the expense. Suppose, for example, that you go to dinner with a business associate. In your industry, what would be the cost of a typical business meal? If you are a truck driver, the typical business meal is going to be different than if you are a movie star or professional athlete. An insurance agent might go to lunch with a client or business associate every day. The key here is that whatever is typical in your industry and your position within the industry is what the IRS will allow as ordinary.

Third, the expense must be necessary. Necessary means that the purpose of the expense is to make more money for your business. It is not enough just to go to lunch with someone and talk business simply because you are friends. Your conservation at lunch must have the intention of increasing the profits in your business.

These three rules are not difficult to meet. Let's say, for example, that your business partner is your spouse. If you are like most business partners, you are always talking about business and always looking for ways to improve your business. Any opportunity you get to have a quiet meal together in a restaurant, make sure you discuss business.

In all cases, just do not be extravagant about meal costs on a regular basis. One rule of thumb here is, "pigs get fat and hogs get slaughtered." If you are greedy and go out to expensive restaurants on a regular basis, the IRS may not look so kindly on your deductions for meals.

Still, I see couples who are always talking about business when they go out to dinner but then forget to pay for their meals with their business credit card. *Big mistake.* Change the facts of your financial life by thinking about these details.

Tax Concept/
S-Corporation Saving
MIKE PINE

The FICA or Self Employment (SE) Tax is a trap. New clients often realize they could have saved tens of thousands of dollars in self-employment taxes had they created a proactive tax plan before tax season.

This simple method of reducing taxes only applies to people who are considered SE. That is, that they receive a portion of their income from somewhere else other than an employer that issues a paycheck and a W-2.

Most small business owners have learned about the pain that SE taxes can cause. But more often than not, professionals such as physicians, attorneys, and, even accountants, are paying SE tax (up to 15.3 percent) in addition to their regular income tax on every dollar of net income they earn. There are blissful ways to legitimately reduce the burden of this tax.

Instead of being a sole proprietor or an LLC for federal tax purposes, all one must do is to make an election to be taxed as an S corporation. At that point, they are then required to pay themselves a "reasonable and customary" wage that is subject to all the payroll taxes. But every dollar earned above that reasonable wage is no longer subject to SE tax.

It is simple and it baffles me every time I see a new client, usually a physician, that has been paying tens of thousands of dollars in unneeded tax. With a few forms, signatures, and setting up a payroll service, you quickly save money.

chapter 6

Entrepreneurs and Investors Get All the Breaks

The government needs to encourage certain activities, and they have two ways of doing that—by force or by policy. But that begs a question: What does the government really want?

Jobs.

Who creates jobs?

Entrepreneurs.

That is why entrepreneurs get all sorts of tax breaks that act as subsidies to encourage job creation.

What else does the government want?

Affordable housing.

Therefore, real estate investors get all sorts of tax breaks that act as subsidies to encourage them to build affordable housing.

Sometimes governments make the mistake of thinking they can create jobs or build housing better than the free market. When that effort fails, they eventually realize that the market does a better job. It costs the government a lot less to give tax benefits to business owners and investors than it does to add jobs or build housing through government-sponsored programs.

Governments get even more specific about the types of investing and jobs they want the market to create by giving specific tax breaks for oil and gas investing, farming and other agriculture, green energy, and low-income housing.

There is a catch, though. To get tax benefits, businesses must be real and intend to make a profit. Paying taxes is less expensive than failing at business. Be sure to get educated before you begin.

Doctors may see themselves as entrepreneurs, even in their status as self-employed independent contractors. And while they do not get punished by the United States government, they also do not receive the lucrative tax incentives and rewards that large businesses or investors get.

If you are a physician elsewhere in the world and want to know what your government really wants to see happen in your country, take a look at your tax laws. Where do all the incentives go? That is where the government wants you to put your money and effort. When you invest in or own companies that function in those areas of government interest, you are doing what the government wants you to do: creating jobs, building housing and other useful buildings, and producing food and energy.

It is so simple, really. When you follow the government's interests and rules, you get substantial tax benefits that you are not receiving now, and that allows you to make and keep more of your money.

As you can tell, I am once again pointing out that abundant gifts await whoever is willing to change their facts of life.

After moving to Texas, my facts of life most definitely needed an overhaul to improve my finances. I had to find a way to shift my earnings out of healthcare and into an area that the United States government incentivized, such as real estate. I began the transformation the year I decided to buy a plot of land and build an apartment community. I figured if I could lease to tenants and stabilize the investment, I could create over $1 million. Of what? Passive income. Net income.

Did I call my representatives and senators to get permission (or assurance) before taking this huge leap in faith? No. Congress already understands that when citizens spend time and money and expend effort to build a business, they need to be rewarded. After all, my investment would produce jobs—for all those skilled construction workers, electricians, and plumbers, and landscapers—and when the complex was completed, it would provide more housing in my community.

There is one more important thing my venture would create: tax revenue for Uncle Sam. It may sound delicious for me to make $1 million on one apartment complex, but my risk would also generate $300,000 in tax revenue for the government, and they did not lift one finger to make it happen. I take that back. Somebody at some point had to pick up a pen and sign all the legislation that provided me and other entrepreneurs with tax breaks.

I can hear you groaning. "That sounds great, but what about me? I work too many hours each week to venture off and develop real estate."

It is true that these business deductions are not available to you now. But they can be yours eventually, and you do not have to buy property and hire an architect to make it happen. All you need to do is start thinking in new ways and consider how you might shift some of your money to income-earning activities outside of healthcare.

It is not that difficult to do. Millions of individuals all over the world have home-based businesses or investments in real estate, energy, or agriculture—and they all enjoy the benefits that come from saving money through the tax code. In the next chapter, I'll show you how to get started.

Tax Concept/ The Home Office Deduction
MIKE PINE

Most doctors do not realize how much work they do at home—after long hours at a health clinic or hospital. I suggest they set up a simple home office and use it as a deduction.

Even if you only use the office to fill out paperwork, educate yourself to do your job better, or for any other "ordinary and necessary" reason, you are eligible for a deduction for the use of that office.

There are some standard requirements: The office must be used predominantly for business and must have an actual door that separates it from the rest of the home.

Although the home office deduction form that must be filed if you are a sole proprietor is considered a "red flag," this can be easily mitigated by setting up a tax entity (like a

PLLC) and having that entity reimburse you for your qualified home office expenses under a Qualified Expense Reimbursement Plan (QERP). By paying for home office expenses through a QERP, the entity is simply taking an office expense, while the taxpayer is receiving a tax-free expense reimbursement and the "red flag" is eliminated.

Some types of eligible home office expenses include depreciation or expensing of office furniture and equipment. Internet, phone, fax, and the proportional share of the home's expenses such as Mortgage Interest, HOA fees, property tax, utilities, maintenance, cleaning, etc.

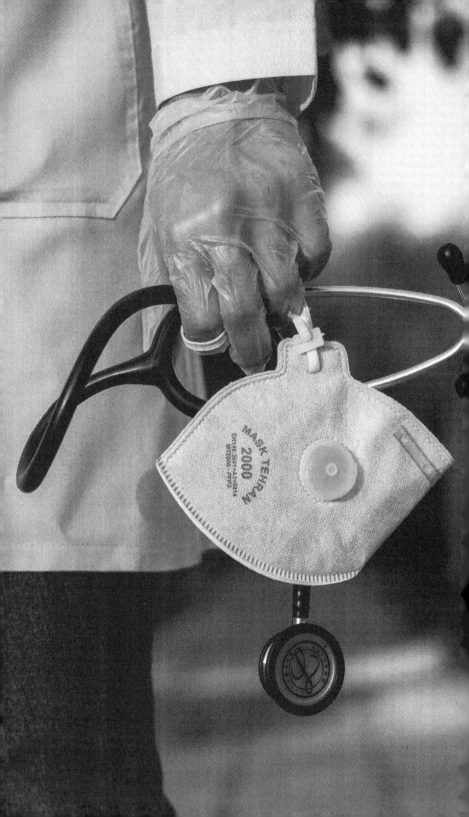

chapter 7

You Can Deduct More Than Just a Stethoscope

Stop being average. Taxes are not fair to the average doctor. But who is the average doctor?

Average doctors have a job, a family, and a mortgage or rent. They get advice from CNN and a local CPA. The average doctor's only available tax benefits are the standard deduction or a few itemized deductions, such as home mortgage interest and charitable contributions. Oh, and, of course, a 401(k) or IRA in the United States to postpone a portion of their tax burden until retirement, which will be average.

The reality is that average doctors have average tax benefits. And as long as they are living the life of an average doctor, there is nothing much I can do for them. There is only one solution: *Stop being average. Change the facts of life. Your life.*

To become an above-average doctor, start doing what the United States government wants you to do—contribute more to the economy. You have the earning power. o Take heart––all you must do now is leverage your salary so that it is more productive.

Once I began to apply my tax knowledge to my own circumstances, I finally understood just how grand things could be. The same will be true for you. Put these new ideas to work immediately and begin to reap the rewards of lower taxes and more cash flow. By taking action, you will increase your understanding of the tax cure and, therefore, be eager to do more to improve your finances.

Once you have become an above-average doctor, you are ready to take the next step toward Dr. Bliss' status. To get there you must choose a path that allows you to deduct almost anything, given the appropriate circumstances. *Anything? How is that possible?* It is how the law works.

Remember this: tax laws favor entrepreneurs and investors because those types of people generally put money into the economy to produce rather than consume. The key to making an expense deductible is to make it a business or investment expense. A simple guideline:

> *If the purpose of the expense is to produce more income, it can be deducted.*

Business expenses are the best kind of deductions. Real estate expenses are the next best, and expenses relating to energy are good as well. Even expenses related to investing in the stock market may be partially deductible, though these are the least deductible because they are not active investments.

So, at the risk of repeating myself, obviously, your first step to becoming a Dr. Bliss and increasing your deductible expenses is to become an entrepreneur or investor. Until you take this step, you will be average and therefore the tax laws will always be stacked against you.

Now is the time to take a deep breath and repeat after me: *I will learn how to become an entrepreneur or investor or both.*

BECOME AN ENTREPRENEUR

Start small. I bought a few rental homes prior to developing an apartment community. It was the slow progression that provided the realization that I could be a successful investor even while practicing medicine.

As my knowledge grew, so did my portfolio and all the tax savings that came with it. I started to realize that I could be the master of my own fate and create the environment I had been longing for—less tax, more wealth. With this newfound knowledge I decided that once I sold the apartment community I had built, I would resign from my practice and seek out new opportunities, not only in real estate but in medicine. As I was headed out the door of my medical group—a shock to my partners—I was offered the position of medical director at a small hospital. At the time, this was a scary venture. *Could I take on that much responsibility?* Since my goal was to exceed average expectations, I accepted the opportunity to feed my passion for learning and growing.

Education is a by-product of taking action and igniting the flame of personal excitement. Success is almost guaranteed when you invest in yourself and your education. As things progressed for me, I began to understand the finance of healthcare in a much more complete way. My expanding knowledge led to me overseeing eight hospitals as a regional medical director and ultimately the group practice president. How could I have predicted all this? I probably could not have. I had to take a big leap by changing the facts of my life or accept and remain frustrated with the status quo.

EDUCATION IGNITES CHANGE

Desperate doctors, male and female, believe they already have earned their credentials, and so they do not seek new horizons-- or they trust there may be a powerful return on their investment if education is expanded beyond medicine. Education changes the facts of your financial life so that great things can happen.

NO RESIGNATION NECESSARY

I am not advocating that you resign from your current position. Rather, I am suggesting that you have a set of marketable skills that you can use to *start your own business*. Start part-time. Set aside space in your home for your business. Do not spend money on a nice office and lots of advertising. Start small, think big. Think about what? Think about the freedom that will come when you can devote most, if not all, of your time to your business, your investments, and your family.

When you start a business, you must put tax planning at the center of your activities. By doing so, your options for deductible expenses will go through the roof. It is easy to make most of your expense deductible when you remember that by spending money your intention is to make even more money. The tax law calls this *having a business purpose for your expenses*.

The next step is to budget your finances. Do not spend money on ridiculous, useless items. Spend it on assets and items that will grow your business. This is called making expenditures that are ordinary in your line of business. Make your expenses count. Make them work for you. When you do that, your expenses become necessary. And when your expenses are necessary, they are deductible.

DOCUMENT EVERYTHING

Keeping accurate books and records is blissful because it means you will not panic when tax time arrives. All successful tax planning requires documentation that clearly indicates your income streams and expenditures. Do not get lazy in this area. Update your bookkeeping at least once a week. The more thorough and accurate your accounting, the better business, and investment decisions you will make. And, of course, you reduce the risk of having difficulties during an audit, if that should occur.

TREAT YOUR NEW ENTERPRISE LIKE A BIG CORPORATION

Although you will start small when launching a new business, treat your enterprise as though it were one of the big dogs like Amazon. Imagine all of the reporting they must do to stay in business and to keep investors, bankers, and management informed about what's going on. You must do the same with your small start-up, even though you are running it from a corner of your home.

Beginning with sound practices ensures that the IRS and other oversight entities do not linger long should an audit be necessary. Accurate financial information also helps you to make wise and informed business and investment decisions.

Best of all, good records will mean every legal expense will be deductible without quarrel from the government. Clear, accurate documentation means you have followed the law exactly as it was meant to be applied.

The result will be lower taxes and less stress. So now you know what I mean when I say that almost every expense can be deductible under the right circumstances. Every time you spend money you can also reduce your taxes, whether it's filling up your car at the gas station, going out to dinner with your spouse and business partner, or even going to Mexico to look at real estate.

Excellent record-keeping indicates you are serious about increasing your wealth. An average taxpayer turns their money over to someone else and hopes and prays that everything works out. You, on the other hand, take responsibility and play an active role in creating wealth and paying as little tax as legally possible.

BECOME AN ACTIVE INVESTOR

Let's suppose you don't want to start a business, but you do want to experience the bliss that comes with being a Dr. Bliss. How can you make that happen?

Become an investor. An active investor, which means you must be an investor who actively invests for the purpose of creating passive income, not earned income.

Passive income is revenue that comes from dividends, rent payments, and successful businesses. This type of income is taxed at a much lower rate than earned income, which comes from appreciation and capital gains, or from your paycheck. *See page 24 for some possible changes on the horizon.* To become a Dr. Bliss, you must find strong investments that create cash flow, otherwise known as passive income.

Does it sound difficult to become an active investor? Banish the thought. Achieving active investor status is quite simple. Just like becoming an entrepreneur, it all starts with your financial education. You don't need a four-year degree in finance. You don't even need a two-year degree, but you do need to take some courses in the type of investing you think you might enjoy. Don't know what you might like? Enroll in a variety of courses that illuminate a variety of investments. There are endless opportunities online.

Once you have an idea of what type of investing you want to do, find a mentor or coach to help you with your investing. *Then start investing.* Along the way, keep track of all of your education and investment expenses, and make sure your tax preparer reports them properly. You should be able to deduct some or all of these expenses on your tax return.

THE PASSIVE INVESTOR

There is one other path to help you become a Dr. Bliss. Learn to be a passive investor. And no, I am not talking about the typical investor who pours money into mutual funds or an exchange-traded fund (ETF).

Instead, invest money with an already active investor who is working directly in business, real estate, agriculture, or energy—the tax-preferred types of investments.

Passive investors also enjoy the benefit of deducting many of their expenses. With the right tax strategy, they can even deduct losses from the investment against the income they earn from other sources.

The key to good passive investing is a good team. You need a great investment advisor and a stellar tax advisor, as well as a good lawyer and a knowledgeable banker. These team members must work together to make sure your best interests are met. A sure way to get team members to collaborate is to hire a wealth strategist. This can be one of the advisors on the team or a separate strategist altogether. The strategist can work to maintain the relationships between you and the other team members.

In many countries, only certain individuals are allowed to be passive investors. In the United States, these individuals are called *accredited* investors. These people meet certain minimum wealth and earning guidelines set up by the government.

The requirements for obtaining accredited investor status as an individual include:

A net worth of over $1 million U.S. at the time the investment is being made	Or, an annual income of over $200,000 U.S. for at least the most recent two years.

Here is the thinking beyond all this: If you have enough money per the guidelines, you likely either have a fairly high financial education and can properly evaluate a deal, or you can afford to lose some of your money on a bad investment without creating financial harm. Sound like you?

While the losses and expenses of a passive investor can be deductible, the rules can be a little tricky. If this route seems right for you, be sure to sit down with your tax advisor to describe what you are planning to be sure you understand the rules and get the full benefit of your expenses and losses. Low fees do not translate into a good deal when it comes to advisors. A good team member is worth their weight in gold. You get what you pay for.

Tax Concept/ Phone it In
MIKE PINE

Do you use a cell phone? Yes, of course, you do. *And*, the need for the phone is both personal and professional. The complication of determining how many minutes are used for medicine may have stopped you from taking this deduction. But the IRS is on your team.

More than a decade ago, the IRS agreed that practically every professional must incur the "ordinary and necessary" expense of a cellular phone and plan. Therefore, the government no longer requires substantiation between personal vs professional use.

If you use a cell phone for business, the IRS will allow your business to deduct 100 percent of the related costs. The size of the deduction may not be as impressive as real estate depreciation. So be it. The goal is to reduce your tax burden, in large and small ways, and by the way, that smartphone you purchased two years ago has depreciated. Deduct the expense.

chapter 8
Real Estate Professional Status

How can you transition from a passive investor to a more tax-savvy active investor and really make huge strides? Become a real estate professional (REP).

The IRS considers you a professional if you are active in the operation of your real estate properties. To achieve this status, every year you must be able to show that you have given at least 750 hours of hands-on involved in your enterprise. This is how you receive 100 percent of the tax breaks we've been discussing. As a full-time physician, this type of commitment may seem out of the question. It was for me, initially. Thankfully, my wife was eager to be involved in changing the facts of our financial life.

All those years ago when I earned my first compensation as a doctor and quickly wrote a fat check to the IRS, I knew something had to change in my life. Micaela had been a schoolteacher; yet, after the birth of our fourth child, we realized that type of job schedule would not work for our family. A real estate professional, however, can set her own hours. And since we were married and filed taxes jointly, Micaela could give the 750 hours needed annually to make our growing business "professional."

First, though, she had to take classes to earn her real estate license. In doing so, she was introduced to the basics of the industry. Once she became a licensed professional in the state of Texas, her status improved. This meant that all our activities both passively and actively in real estate depreciation could be used for all our income via our combined 1040 tax filling. This gave us the opportunity to reduce my W2 income from my medical career while allowing us to make huge gains in our financial lives.

There are two main hurdles a taxpayer must overcome to qualify for real estate professional (REP) status.

First, an individual must spend at least 750 hours in the tax year performing "Real Estate Professional Activities" (REPAs). Micaela, for example, had to achieve the 750-hour threshold on her own; married taxpayers cannot "pool" their hours. REP activities are loosely defined and very much a grey area in tax law. The IRS has no comprehensive listing of what activities qualify. However, the IRS does say that qualifying real estate activities include property development, redevelopment, construction, reconstruction, acquisition, conversion, rental, operation, management, leasing, or brokerage trade or business.

Some activities obviously fall into the approved category:

> Time spent studying for a real estate license

> Time spent finding and making listings

> Time spent showing properties and marketing their business

> Time spent on all directly related travel

Beyond the activities listed above, things get complicated. The IRS says that a low-level accountant for a real estate management company that gets paid via W-2 does not qualify as a REP. Yet, a manager of real estate properties that also gets paid via W-2 can qualify, which suggests that a senior-level accounting executive at a similar management firm may very well qualify.

Second, after qualifying under the 750-hour rule, the taxpayer must prove that more time was spent performing REPAs than any other professional activity. That's tough on a full-time practicing physician who spends 1,800 hours each year treating patients. To qualify, the doctor would need to spend at least 1801 hours performing REPAs.

But maybe you are a physician who has developed real estate income and, therefore, can reduce the number of hours spent practicing medicine. In that case, your REPA hours may be greater than your medical professional hours.

One of my partners is a great example of achieving the REP balancing act. Although a practicing periodontist, to expand real estate hours, this doctor has created a blog on real estate investing that helps others succeed with rental properties which is directly related to him growing his real estate earnings. He also earns equity in real estate properties that he helps manage. In addition to constantly blogging, my partner speaks with potential investors and budding real estate professionals that may invest in some of the entities he helps to manage. The hours add up quickly, and he keeps a record of all the time he spends in his real estate profession so that he easily fulfilled the 750-hour minimum, which is more than the hours he gives to his periodontal practice.

To be sure, the guy doesn't get much sleep. However, he rests easy knowing that he can easily prove that he qualifies for REP status—and thus earn the amazing tax benefits.

Here is one last example concerning a spouse who may help manage multiple rental properties and keeps a part-time job unrelated to real estate: they must log at least 750 hours managing assets—and those hours must exceed the time spent at the part-time job.

Micaela earned her license quickly and is now an integral part of our business success.

But what if you are a busy doctor and your significant other cannot achieve REP status?

Mike Pine can explain it best.

Tax Concept/ REP with Short-Term Rentals
◇ MIKE PINE

If you are unable to attain REP status, consider taking advantage of depreciation using short-term or vacation rental property ownership. First, let's discuss some complications.

Many people got involved with short-term rentals through sites such as Airbnb and VRBO. Initially, time spent operating these types of rentals was used by some taxpayers to qualify for REP status. Then the IRS put a stop to that by applying a rule that stated any rental property operating over a tax year with shorter than a 7-day average lease period, does not qualify as a rental activity for REP purposes. This led to an unintended consequence: if the short-term rentals don't qualify as real estate activities, then by default, they qualify as standard trade or business operations.

Any taxpayer that operates a trade or business, and "materially participates" under the passive activity rules of the Internal Revenue Cod Section 469, is allowed to deduct net taxable losses from their business against their other sources of ordinary income (subject to at-risk and basis limitations). Thankfully, you can very likely qualify as a material participant in any trade or business with an hourly threshold of only 500 hours per tax year.

Additionally, couples may *combine* their time to meet the 500-hour requirement. Yet, there is an additional hurdle: to meet material participation safe harbor requirements a taxpayer with multiple similar businesses, must spend at least 100 hours on each business entity.

One more wrinkle. The short-term rental rules further evolved. Taxpayers now need to spend more time on each individual property than any other individual or business entity.

For instance, if a taxpayer owns five short-term rentals, spends 101 hours working on each but uses a management company that spends more than 101 hours on each of the same properties, the taxpayer would not qualify for each activity and therefore would not be able to utilize net taxable losses to offset their other active income. If, however, using the same facts except that the management company only spent 99 hours on each property, the taxpayer would then qualify as a "material participant."

These "safe harbor" hurdles allow a taxpayer to enjoy the tax benefits of net taxable losses while facing lowered risk that the IRS would challenge them. However, the actual IRS rules regarding whether or not someone is a "material participant" are even less stringent, but utilizing the less stringent hurdles incurs greater risk with the IRS. It is always better to be bulletproof rather than bullet resistant.

As mentioned, a taxpayer must also meet the basis and at-risk requirements. These two concepts can get pretty complex but in general, can be explained in a relatively simple manner.

BASIS LIMITATION: To have basis in a property in order to take a taxable loss, the taxpayer must have put enough cash, and/or debt that is greater than or equal to the cumulative losses that they want to take on their tax returns. As debt is concerned, in order for it to provide *basis*, it must either be recourse debt to the taxpayer or be "Qualified Non-Recourse Debt" (QNR). Real property debt that utilizes the property in question as collateral and is not recourse to the taxpayer, i.e., a typical mortgage, is Qualified Non-Recourse Debt.

AT-RISK LIMITATION: The taxpayer must bear an economic risk if the property were to be taken from them. In nearly all situations where a taxpayer would own a short-term rental, such economic risk exists and, therefore, a taxpayer would meet the at-risk limitations.

For example, say Jane and John purchased a vacation rental property in 2021 on Destin beach for $1,000,000 by paying $200,000 in cash and getting a mortgage for the additional $800,000. Jane and John then spent 4 weeks working on renovating and decorating the property while working 8 hours per day 5 days per week. This would mean that both Jane and John spent 160 hours for a combined 320 hours. Then, during the year they both spend an additional combined 200 hours working to list the property online, making reservations, talking with renters. The average lease period for the year was 6.5

days. This would mean that Jane and John accumulated 520 total hours operating their short-term rental business in 2021.

Further, assume that they did list the property through some management companies that stated their people only spent a total of 200 hours managing the property (or replace the management company with a cleaning service). Since John and Jane combined meet the 500-hour material participation hurdle, and the management company spent less time than they did, they could take any net taxable loss for the year to offset their other active income from their day jobs.

Next, suppose that they engaged a cost segregation firm to provide a report that stated 30 percent of their property's cost was attributable to the property with a 15-year or less tax depreciation life. Presume that the actual rental activities had operating expenses equal to the rental income and, therefore, operated at break even. In such a case, even though they only paid $200,000 cash, they would receive a tax deduction of $300,000 during the first year of operating the ST Rental, assuming that "Bonus Depreciation remains enacted." If John and Jane's actual income tax rate is 37 percent, they would save $111,000 in taxes for 2021, while also having purchased and built a vacation rental business that will provide income for years to come. Imagine that, paying $200,000 and getting $111,000 back in taxes, meaning they got a million-dollar vacation rental for a net out-of-pocket cost of $89,000!

Now assume in year two that John and Jane decide to buy another vacation rental under similar facts as the first one. They would want to make sure that they still materially participate in the first property by spending a combined 100 hours without allowing anyone to spend more time than them, and make sure they spend enough time on the second one so that their combined hours spent on their budding new short-term business exceeded the 500-hour hurdle, and they could then find themselves with another 100+K tax savings. They would also have two properties in two years that were paying for themselves. The power to snowball such activities into a large portfolio of vacation rentals over a short period of time is extraordinary!

chapter 9
Expanding Depreciation

Now that you have considered the idea of creating a small business that improves your goal of lowering your taxes, let's get back to the subject of depreciation in real estate. Ownership may seem challenging at first. But my first home profoundly changed the facts of my financial life.

After my residency in Indianapolis, my wife and I decided to keep the home we had purchased as a rental property. That became our little home-based business outside of medicine. It was easy to operate, we learned a lot, and by renting one single-family home we gained enough confidence to expand.

By the time we moved to Texas, the 2008 mortgage crisis had forced many homeowners to foreclose on their properties. Valuations plummeted, and new homes that did not require a lot of upgrades could be purchased at incredibly low prices. And, there was very little competition because the downturn had created a glut in the market.

We eventually owned seven homes in the Houston area and enjoyed the tax reductions each provided. There was also passive income involved, and I know other investors who are quite pleased with this strategy for expanding wealth and tax benefits. In fact, my realtor in Indianapolis who remains a good friend set himself up quite nicely this way.

Now consider the various tax reductions available to us and others who invest this way:

Mortgage interest payments on loans used to acquire or fix up rental properties

Interest on credit cards to purchase services for the rental activity

Repairs to gutters, floors, roofs, replacing broken windows, etc.

Personal property, such as furniture or garden equipment used on the rental properties

A relatively new pass-through tax deduction (scheduled to expire in 2025). Until then, some landlords may be allowed to deduct 20 percent of their net rental income or 2.5 percent of the initial cost of their rental property

Hiring service personnel for rental homes, such as yard maintenance and landscapers, etc.	Mileage to address tenant complaints, for example, while I did not live in Houston, when I drove there, I was allowed to deduct the mileage.

For a time, I very much appreciated the advantages of owning multiple single-family homes. It was an important step in my education. But I eventually began to feel frustrated. Although Houston was a market with great opportunities, and I delegated maintenance and other responsibilities to local businesses, it became untenable to operate those properties from afar. After all, I was a practicing physician with ample responsibilities. The inconveniences eventually led me to utter these infamous words: *There must be a better way.*

Then, another thought soon followed: *Could the "better way" include even more tax deductions?* Yes. But my ability to take full advantage would not happen until after I survived a double mortgage nightmare.

Micaela and I decided we needed a change. The plan involved my leaving the exhausting medical practice that had brought us to Texas, and moving our family to a larger real estate market, where we hoped to find more investment opportunities. To make all that happen, we sold our rental properties in Houston, bought a new home for us, and accepted an offer to buy the home we were living in. That seemed like a good plan until the sale of our previous residence collapsed the day before closing. That meant we were stuck with paying two mortgages until we could find another buyer.

When fighting through adversity, it is difficult to be objective. Years later we looked back and said, "Ah, there was a lesson in all that travail." In this case, there was also the humbling realization that I had made the very mistake I had often criticized other doctors for making: Overextending themselves to buy the biggest house on the block so that they would have a larger mortgage tax deduction.

For 18 months I suffered the pain of a hefty mortgage payment on two residences. It was an instructive contrast to owning rental homes. I swore I would never let that happen again.

The double-trouble mortgages were also a reminder that I was able to withstand the economic challenge only because I had purchased and profited from rental properties. Along the way, I had enjoyed some very tasty tax deductions.

Let's stop here for a moment. The facts of your financial life will change more than once. No worries. That is a sure sign that you are continuing to learn and grow.

EXPAND YOUR DEPRECIATION

The purchase of seven single-family homes provided a new way to increase my income. I would simply raise the rent on each property. You might think this gave me a sense of power. I saw it more as financial creativity. The math was simple but profound when raising rents by $100:

$$7 \times \$100 = \$700 \text{ per month} \times 12 \text{ months} = \$8,400 \text{ annual increase.}$$

That is a nice little equation.

Let's not forget, though, that my enthusiasm for those numbers eventually wore thin. Perhaps, it was only a matter of satisfying my temperament, which may be quite different than yours but finding a better way to proceed demanded some new rules. In other words, I had to change the facts of my financial life.

First, when buying multiple single-family homes, it is unlikely that they will all be clustered in the same neighborhood. Therefore, when paying visits to Houston, I had more than one stop. *Enough already. Why not have many units under one roof?*

Also, while the multiplication example above looks sweet, expanding the number of units I owned gave me an even better result:

$$50 \times \$100 \text{ per month} =$$
$$\$5,000 \text{ per month} \times 12 \text{ months} = \$60,000$$

Obviously, to achieve that kind of expansion, I would need to operate in a whole new arena—apartment buildings, otherwise known as multifamily commercial real estate. And not just one building, but eventually many properties. The income would increase, but let's not forget the diamond in rough: depreciation. That too would multiply.

I repeat, how much money you earn each year is important, but it is surpassed by how much money you retain. The legal deductions provided by depreciation in a small or large apartment complex will do wonders for your tax-cut taste buds.My first foray into multifamily complexes, admittedly, created more headaches than hallelujahs in the early going. I purchased a three-acre city lot that was a remnant from a foreclosure. As I said, I decided to build an apartment building. Although the sale of my seven single-family homes gave me some money to work with, some of that was tied up during my fiasco paying mortgages on two residences. So, to take the leap into apartment ownership, I needed investors, and I was not too proud to enlist my brother. I drove him to the site of my big dream. He stared at the land with a blank face.

"You're going to do what?" Tim asked.

"Build an apartment complex," I answered.

"You're crazy."

As I earned my degree in the school of hard knocks, I was more and more inclined to agree with him.

Land development demanded a whole other set of skills than those required to merely own a building. I made numerous mistakes as I learned the ramifications of city codes, zoning, and certificates of occupancy. hen I personally took on the enormous task of leasing each unit. Through it all, there were many sleepless nights and moments of extreme worry.

There was a happy ending, however, because, in fact, my venture may have been crazy but it was also a new way of looking at finance. My three-acre extravaganza sold for a profit which gave Tim and me some of the seed money we needed to co-found Napali Capital, which enabled us to make bigger deals for buildings that exponentially expanded our tax benefits from depreciation.

DEPRECIATION NATION

When purchasing computers and other physical office assets the business owner knows the equipment will lose value through the years. Fortunately, the depreciation can be deducted when tax time comes along.

Although this same type of deduction is available to owners of real estate, it is not immediately recognized as an important reason for buying homes and commercial buildings. We do not realize that we could rename our country Depreciation Nation, because everywhere you travel, you will see fine, impressive buildings that are deprecating but not necessarily losing value. Compare that to the laptop on your desk that you will never be able to resell at a price higher than the original cost. (This is a subtle reminder to curb your enthusiasm for buying expensive equipment for your home business office.)

Obviously, when investing in physical assets, we want to see an increase in value. Yet, the paradox in real estate is that while improving a multifamily building, depreciation plays a big role in growing wealth because it lowers taxes. You keep more of what you earn.

Let's stay with the example of an apartment building that includes multiple living units. You cover the cost of the property by collecting rents and payment for other services on site. You may decide to make improvements

that cost money. Plus, even if you do not spend ⸌
you can still benefit from depreciation. No, you did not
have to buy anything, such as a computer, so that your
business could claim a deduction. There were no out-
of-pocket expenses, in this example, depreciation is
still part of the equation.

These days, depreciation for commercial buildings
in the United States spans 39 years at a rate of about
2.5 percent.

Before calculating depreciation, you must deduct
the value of the land. For example, you have purchased
a $2 million commercial building, but that value drops
to $1.56 million after subtracting the land value. Even
so, this would allow you a depreciation deduction of
about $40,000 each year for 39 years.

A smaller commercial property of $500,000 would
be allowed an annual depreciation deduction of
$10,000 each year for 39 years. Get the picture?

Depreciation is not your only deduction, but it
is a significant gift that doctors may overlook when
considering a new investment. Too often the doctor
thinks in terms of deducting interest on the loan or
the money spent on maintaining the building. Think
again, because there is another advantage: Even if
you borrowed the entire price of the buildings, in other
words, the bank's money bought the building, you still
get the depreciation allowed for the full cost of the
building.

2.5% / million grey 20K
depreciation / yr
for 36 years

Faster depreciation happens when you itemize everything inside the structure. Imagine a typical kitchen or bathroom, and the floor coverings in hallways and the lobby fixtures. Are there improvements that have been made to the exterior of the building or in a pool area or parking lot? All these items are deductions, and they depreciate faster than the structure itself.

So, when you eagerly dream of selling your building for a profit—years hence—do not forget to fully appreciate the financial advantages that real estate ownership offers throughout your time of ownership.

Also, take your deductions as soon as possible. An experienced tax advisor can help with the timetable. Remember, the tax code was written to encourage the investor to do more with their money. The more cash you free up as the result of depreciation, the more you must spend on further improvements or the purchase of other assets.

But how do you speed up your depreciation deductions?

Tax Concept/
Never Fear IRS Audit
MIKE PINE

The tax cure assesses tax on net income, meaning any reasonable expense that is incurred in generating income is tax-deductible. This applies to businesses and, as of 2017, is no longer applicable to taxpayers who earn all their income via a W-2.

When meeting with new clients, I find that many of their tax decisions have been made on the basis of fear of an IRS audit. I get it. No one wants to get audited by the IRS. But that fear should not cause you to pay *more* taxes than you are legally obligated to pay.

A good tax partner will help assuage the fear by providing you with good record-keeping systems to both establish, and defend if needed, the basis for all of your reasonable and legal tax deductions.

In essence, a good tax partner will prepare an audit defense file with your annually prepared tax returns. If you have such a tax partner, although an audit can still be a headache, you will already have all the needed documentation to defend your tax return. And a good tax partner will have made you familiar with any tax position that might be challenged while providing you a risk-versus-reward analysis so you don't get any surprises.

Don't get me wrong, I do think it is important to avoid IRS "Red Flags" as much as possible. But it is more important to take advantage of the tax deductions you are eligible for.

chapter 10

Cost Segregation for More Tax Relief

To speed up deductions, the real estate investor must break down the total property value into categories, and then cherry-pick the fastest ones.

If you have 50 rental units, and each includes kitchen cabinets, sinks, and toilets, those things equal a percentage of the property value. *Since these things depreciate faster,* you can increase the normal 2.5 percent depreciation deduction to 10 or 15 percent. Maybe higher. All of which puts more money in your pocket by reducing your tax bill. And remember, many of these benefits can recur, year after year.

This is why paying close attention to taxation on real estate is a game-changer. When purchasing a property, it is common sense for the buyer to assess everything from the basement to the roof to accurately appraise its value. The same due diligence should be applied to understanding the tax code as it pertains to your investments. Unfortunately, many real estate investors simply buy a building, subtract out the value of the land, and deduct depreciation based on 27.5 years for residential real estate and 39 years for non-residential real estate.

Bliss, however, is a result of understanding the rules surrounding depreciation. Smart investors know that the IRS sets the depreciable life for items such as appliances at five years, furniture and fixtures have a seven-year life, and items that qualify as "leasehold improvements" are recovered over 15 years.

The IRS also knows that when buying large or multi-unit properties, it is difficult to segregate the above-mentioned items from the building itself, so it has made a compromise to allow for acceptable methodology to simply break out a fair estimate of those items and then allow their costs to be recovered over the faster periods. So the smart investor buys a property, engages an engineer that specializes in cost segregation studies, and gets a large portion of the building's purchase price allocated to shorter life assets. This means the Dr. Bliss investor greatly multiplies the depreciation deduction early in the life of the investment.

As I mentioned previously, an engineer that specializes in cost segregation a/k/a cost seg specialist) is an integral part of maximizing your tax benefits. A qualified cost seg specialist will be familiar with the IRS' requirements, aggressively segregate out all shorter life assets, and provide your CPA with a report that not only includes the amounts that can be deducted more quickly but also will hold up against any IRS scrutiny. When determining who to use for the study, find someone who has a lot of experience in performing real estate cost segregations studies. Be sure to ask these questions: Has their work ever undergone any IRS scrutiny? If so, what was the result? If done properly, a cost segregation study is practically bulletproof with the IRS. The study will have followed IRS prescribed methodology and shut down any concerns by the IRS.

Engineering studies are essential when you realize that categorizing depreciation deductions is like sending an invoice to the government, knowing that it will be paid immediately. This is another reason I often repeat three little words—*I love taxes.* As we profit from real estate, our tax bill does not increase but instead decreases. We are being paid for our enterprise.

For doctors, the benefits cannot be overstated, especially since we know the laws are not friendly to us. We must learn about taxation and take every deduction we are entitled to. And if this is one more responsibility for men and women who are already heavily burdened, we must also assess the cost of financial illiteracy.

I work with an excellent tax partner who has been a tremendous help to me through the years. Occasionally, he will notice that a new client is not taking some depreciation deductions. Usually, this is because the value of the real estate has not been itemized in the way I explained above. These types of oversights are a reminder that taxation is not a generality. Specifics can significantly improve a tax return and therefore your cash flow. As a doctor, you would not generally prescribe antibiotics or other medicines. So, do not do it with your money.

This is all second nature to Dr. Bliss. He buys a commercial apartment building knowing the magic of depreciation will aid him greatly now and over the future, depending on the type of building he has purchased and the country in which he lives. He is allowed these deductions even though his building is healthy and may increase in value.

The blissful doctor is a smart investor because he or she also knows building costs are covered by the cash flow the building generates through rent. The doctor is not really paying anything out of pocket for the property and might even be making a profit each year. Despite all this, the doctor is entitled to take advantage of depreciation.

Let's look at another example of depreciation.

The investor pays $1 million for a building but subtracts the land value of $200,000 and that leaves $800,000 to depreciate—each year. How much the doctor is allowed to deduct depends on how fast the government will let him depreciate the building.

Since commercial buildings are now depreciated over 39 years, he gets the blissful deduction each year of $20,500.

$800,000 ÷ 39 years, for about 2.5 percent per year

You may be wondering about the interest expense for the loan to buy a building or out-of-pocket expenses associated with maintenance. That is smart to be thinking that way. But those expenses are also deductible.

As amazing as it may seem, the actual cost of the building is a non-cash expense (an expense that doesn't reduce your cash flow) that gives you a deduction. Even better, you do not only get a deduction for the money you put into the building, but you also get a deduction for the money the bank loaned you. To repeat, you get a depreciation deduction for the entire cost of the building, as mentioned in the previous chapter.

Am I boring you with repetition? I hope not. My reason for testing your patience is my belief that repetition is a good teacher. When learning medical procedures, a new doctor may be confronted with the adage, *Watch one, Do one, Teach one.* But I'd rather learn from multiple examples.

So please bear with me as I remind you that Dr. Bliss never just buys a building. He also buys everything inside the building and the landscaping and other exterior components, such as protective fencing and the parking lot. He bought the floor coverings, the window coverings, the cabinetry, and so on.

That means a portion of the $800,000 price tag applies specifically to all of the above. When you hear a colleague say, "I'm thinking of buying a building," I want you to visualize more than the artifice. See everything inside each apartment and smile, because all that stuff is the fast food of depreciation.

Let's go further. Of the $800,000 building price, $100,000 really belongs to the cabinets, floor coverings, window coverings, and other things that came with the building. As you now know, this $100,000 is depreciated much faster than the building itself. So instead of getting a 2.5 to 5 percent deduction each year, as shown in the math example above, the wise investor will get a 20 percent or more deduction each year for this $100,000 portion of his purchase until it is fully depreciated. Add another $20,000 in annual deductions.

So, the doctor bought a one-million-dollar property. The land has a fair value of $200,000, meaning everything on the land has a value of the remaining $800,000. An engineer specializing in cost segregation provides a detailed study of the property and determines that the building itself is worth $700,000 and all the items inside and around it, which the IRS allows to be depreciated over five years, is worth $100,000. So now you get two segregated components of the non-land value to depreciate:

- Building: $700,000 over 39 years, or $18,000 per year
- Other tangible assets: $100,000 over 5 years, or $20,000 per year

The total annual depreciation of the two segregated components is now $38,000 per year for the first five years. The investor nearly doubled his annual depreciation deduction simply by knowing the law and hiring an engineer.

This example is uber-conservative and the actual annual depreciation deduction would likely be two to three times as much, thus helping the doctor who invested this way lead a very blissful life. In many cases, the investor is able to deduct more in the first few years than the cash down payment for the property.

Tax Concept/ Cost Segregations
MIKE PINE

Cost segregations are specifically sanctioned by the IRS and technically required by law. The IRS doesn't enforce the requirement because it means less revenue for them, and the IRS knows that the lazier the taxpayer and/or accountant, the more revenue the United States Treasury makes.

According to the IRS audit guide, there are specific allowable cost segregation methodologies. These allowable methodologies are complicated and can't just be a best guess. You can either use engineers or CPAs that are specifically qualified and well versed in the IRS allowable methods. You don't have to do it when you first buy the property. This allows for some great tax planning, as you want to do the cost segregation in a year when you are in the highest tax bracket so that you get the most tax benefits; however, recent legislation has incentivized owners to cost segregate in the first year allowing huge allocations for bonus depreciation, thus encouraging investors to place more capital in the system!

Remember that depreciation is a deduction, not a credit, so your benefit is based on your tax bracket. A deduction in a high tax bracket is always better than a deduction in a low tax bracket. When you do a cost segregation, no matter how many years later, you get to catch up on all the depreciation you would have taken if you had done your cost segregation in the year you purchased the property. So, if you have owned the property for several years, you will have a lot of extra deductions in the year you do the cost segregation.

Let's explore two examples:
The first one is that you purchase a single-family residence to rent long-term. Assume you pay $1,000,000 for the property, with the land being worth $100,000. Also, assume that you don't make any improvements or buy any additional furnishings. If you don't perform a cost segregation study, you would be able to depreciate the $900,000 of cost

allocated to the house over 27.5 years as "residential real estate." That would equate to an annual depreciation deduction of nearly $33,000 ($900,000 / 27.5). If you do get a cost segregation study in the first year, let's assume that the cost seg specialist is able to segregate 25 percent of the building to the property with a 7-year tax life (i.e., flooring and similar items). In the first year, you would have two components of depreciation:

1) **Building (900,000 * 75 percent) = $675,000 depreciated over 27.5 years for an annual total depreciation deduction of nearly $25,000.**

2) **7- year life assets (900,000 * 25 percent) = $225,000 depreciated over 7 years for an additional annual total depreciation deduction of $32,000**

This means that the annual depreciation over the first 7 years would be $57,000. However, if 100 percent bonus depreciation is available as it is at the time of this writing, you would get an immediate bonus depreciation deduction in the first year of $225,000 + the annual regular depreciation of $25,000 for a total first-year depreciation deduction of $250,000!

For the second example, let's assume the same fact sets as the first one, however, you don't perform a cost segregation study until the end of the 7th year after you placed the rental on the market. So for the first 7 years, you received a standard deduction.

• **Building (900,000 * 100 percent) = $900,000 depreciated over 27.5 years for an annual total depreciation deduction of nearly $33,000.**

1) This would equate to total depreciation deductions of $231,000 over the first 7 years. ($33,000 * 7 years)

But at the end of the 7th year, you determine to have cost segregation performed that works out to the same percentages of the study performed in the first example. The IRS then allows you to deduct all of the depreciation deductions that you could have received had you performed the cost segregation in year one. As explained in the prior example, if you had performed the segregation in the first year, your annual depreciation expense for the first seven years would have been:

Building (900,000 * 75 percent) = $675,000 depreciated over 27.5 years for an annual total depreciation deduction of nearly $25,000.

7- year life assets (900,000 * 25 percent) = $225,000 depreciated over 7 years for an additional annual total depreciation deduction of $32,000

This would have provided a total annual depreciation deduction of $57,000, for a total deduction over the first seven years of ($57,000 * 7 years) = $399,000. And because you only took a $231,000 deduction over the first 7 years, the IRS would allow you to "catch up" the depreciation you missed out on for an additional deduction in year 7 of ($399,000 - $231,000) = $168,000!

Having waited until the 7th year to perform the cost segregation would have been a fantastic tax planning tool if your income tax rate in year 7 was significantly higher than in year one. Although, you would have potentially missed out on the seven years of earnings from the initial tax savings you would have realized in the first year. Again, this illustrates once again why it is important to plan your taxes and consider all the pros and cons, always proactively.

PART 2
Borrow, Protect, Retire

chapter 11

The Loan Toolbox

If you decide to make real estate a fact of your financial life, you may need to consider taking on some debt. But let's make sure it is the right kind of debt. Debt is a tool to be used to create wealth. It is imperative to break any mindset that debt is bad. Using debt and leverage creates tax benefits for the full amount of the property, while not just the amount we are invested. We in essence are "double-dipping," and we are getting all the breaks and benefits with a minimal amount of down payment or capital. That's leverage!!

We accept a loan to help us achieve goals we cannot fulfill on our own. Even the wealthiest people in the world are familiar with debt. What separates winners and losers is how debt is employed. Money is not a number; it is a tool. When you want to change a lock on the door, you do not show up with a sledgehammer.

 Bad debt is the misuse of a lending tool. Credit cards are the most obvious example because they are an addictive convenience and a trap. Car loans and leases are not much better, even though vehicles are a necessity. But do we really need the hottest car on the lot?

Chronic bad debt pain is caused by a lending tool that is too heavy to handle. You may love your enormous, expensive house—until the payment is due. The wrong choice can hurt us in at least two different ways:

> **1. Large monthly payments create a financial strain on monthly expenses.**

> **2. Small monthly payments are easy to meet and barely pay down the principal. As a result, the agreement lasts for decades and the cradle-to-grave cost far exceeds the amount of money originally borrowed.**

Bad debt that lingers also damages credit ratings which makes it difficult to acquire the appropriate lending tool when you come upon a wiser investment opportunity.

What about student debt? Many doctors are familiar with the hobbling obligation to pay education loans. At least those of us who accepted a loan improved our professional status and potential earning power by attending college and medical school. The tool we used was effective, in most cases, and is an example of good debt: Money borrowed to purchase an essential need and fulfill a goal.

My goal after becoming a doctor was financial freedom. I quickly learned that merely borrowing money to buy single-family homes and then commercial real estate was not the way to go. Just like the surgeon who understands the risks each operation entails, I had to learn more about the financial tools within my reach, as Dr. Bliss did at the start of his investment career.

YOUR TOOLBOX

The toolbox analogy is useful because we need more than one instrument to succeed in wealth creation. Your toolbox is a diverse mix of possibilities because your real estate portfolio will likely also be diverse.

All real estate assets and other investments deals will be structured differently, so naturally, we will need appropriate options to get things done properly. For example, an older apartment complex may need a large rehab to upgrade its position in the market. You already have a mortgage on the property, and you will increase cash flow by improving each unit. So, what tool do you reach for? A bridge loan, most likely.

A bridge loan, sometimes called a swing loan, might be needed for a couple of weeks or up to three years. In some cases, it might be used to keep you afloat pending a long-term financing deal. Think of this type of loan as a conduit. When buying commercial real estate, though, you will typically consider government-backed Fannie Mae and Freddie Mac loans. They are the simplest way to finance multifamily properties on a larger scale with a minimal amount of risk, in my opinion. Both were created by the government to boost the housing market.

Fannie Mae stands for the Federal National Mortgage Association. Freddie Mac is the Federal Home Loan Mortgage Corporation.

Both organizations target certain markets. Fannie Mae buys mortgages from large retail banks while Freddie Mac buys only from smaller institutions. But here is the key: Both entities help banks make a lot more loans while keeping interest rates low. Sound like an effective lending tool? You bet.

Not that Fannie and Freddie have not had some challenges along the way. They saved the U.S. housing market following its crisis in 2008. To stabilize that troubling time, Fannie Mae and Freddie Mac eventually offered about 90 percent of the financing for new mortgages, which meant they doubled their piece of the mortgage market. Why? Financing from private banks had been frozen.. They could not take on any more risk. Even after the recession, banks were unlikely to offer a loan unless it came with Fannie Mae and Freddie Mac guarantees.

Fannie and Freddie are not the only powerful loan options in your toolbox. You might consider commercial mortgage-backed securities (CMBS). This is a fixed-income security that is collateralized by commercial real estate loans for office buildings, hotels, apartment complexes, etc.

A CMBS is not merely the loan you have been given. The bank bundles groups of its loans and then sells them to investors as a series of bonds. In other words, your loan combined with others has been turned into products, which range from the highest-rated and therefore lowest-risk CMBS to the highest risk (with potential for big gains) and lowest rating.

By the way, the securities I mentioned above may frighten you if you remember the damage done by the 2008 mortgage crash. But the problem was RMBS (residential mortgage-backed securities), not CMBS securities. RMBS securities were sold with an A rating when, in fact, they were a collection of highly at-risk mortgage holders who were ridiculously over-leveraged. It was a game of cards destined to collapse.

Even so, there are important differences between CMBS and Fannie/Freddie loans.

Whereas Fannie and Freddie are backed by the government, the CMBS loans are privately backed by the investors who purchase the securities created by the banks. This leads us to the terms *recourse* and *non-recourse.*

If you default on a CMBS loan, the investors can force you to pay it back, even after seizing the collateral involved in the deal. Non-recourse loans offer investors fewer ways of recouping a debt gone bad. That is why Fannie and Freddie loans are less risky.

Here is another way to think about non-recourse and recourse loans. Each type suggests a relationship. The CMBS is serviced on behalf of bondholders who are absolutely guaranteed their money. If your project is in trouble and you need to discuss forbearance or some sort of relief, do not expect cooperation from strangers who are bondholders.

Conversely, if you have a non-recourse loan that is in trouble, you may very well have a relationship with the bank official who helped set up the deal. You can call up that person and say, "Listen, we're in a bind. We need 90 days of interest only, or we need a payment deferral. Can we talk?" Thankfully, that bank has a vested interest and may not want to hold the asset, but they are also not necessarily going to come after you either. You have a relationship.

Bridge loans are non-recourse too. But keep in mind, the banks will usually be aggressive about setting higher fees and interest rates.

Another lending source is insurance companies that have large dormant pools of money. Multifamily properties are a way to keep those funds working so that they generate income.

With all these choices, how does the passive income physician make the best decision? One more facet to remember is leverage.

To use my example of upgrading an apartment complex, when I secured a bridge loan, the loan was based on the value of that property. A bridge lender may be willing to offer up to 90 percent of the asset. That is a lot of leverage. It means for only 10 percent you are controlling a large piece of cash. On the other hand, a CMBS loan may only cover 60 percent of the property value. This diminishes the leverage because you must front four times as much money to get that loan.

Your circumstances, and the wisdom of your partners, will help you determine which tool is best for your project. Leverage is a powerful thing when it works in your favor, and a crushing factor when it works against you.

SHIELDING THE PASSIVE INCOME INVESTOR

In the beginning, passive income investors are shielded from these types of risks. Decisions about such loans may be years away. In the beginning, you will simply be browsing for strong ways to grow your money but will not be leading the charge on the purchase of a multifamily property.

Regardless, start getting comfortable with your loan toolbox even when you are basically just window shopping. It is a bit like the novice trader who is watching the stock market perform without skin in the game. By educating yourself while on the sidelines, you will develop a sense of which tool to reach for, depending on the structure of any given deal. And more importantly, understand other investments that you may be making in any financial sector.

Mostly, you must understand your exposure to risk before you invest. In this way, you develop the caution of a carpenter who would most likely assess a home improvement challenge before wielding an ax or a screwdriver.

You have almost a limitless number of options: government-backed loans, bank loans, secondary market, securitized bonds, and private-investor loans. Short-term and long-term. Non-recourse and recourse. And then there is leverage, that awesome force of finance. Use them all wisely.

Tax Concept/ Remember Credits

MIKE PINE

Tax credits are much more powerful than deductions. If you are paying the top marginal 37 percent tax rate, a $100 deduction saves you only $37. But a $100 credit reduces your tax by that entire amount—$100.

IMPORTANT TAX CREDITS INCLUDE:

▶ Child tax credit

▶ General business credits

▶ Research and Development is huge and greatly underutilized

▶ Work opportunity credits

▶ Tip credits

▶ Electric vehicle credits

▶ Small business stock, while not exactly a credit, is an amazing opportunity and rarely used.

chapter 12

Asset Protection

True freedom is spending your time any way you wish. This means you have money in the bank and grows from streams of passive income. You don't have to worry about the price of a new car, personal trainer, or your mortgage payment. For me, it also means taking an annual family trip to Kauai.

In the past, I was not living in freedom. Like many of you, I spent weekends, nights, and holidays in a hospital emergency room. After sacrificing years of my life and lots of money on higher education to learn my profession, I felt exhausted and sometimes paralyzed when I thought about my future. Despite all the years of training, I felt trapped with no alternatives. This was terrifying because I was not sure I could or should continue to tread the medical path I had chosen. If I changed directions, how would I support my family, pay a mortgage and my medical school debt?

Only in recent years have I been able to step back and take a deep breath. Finally, I had enough assets to pay my expenses without working every day. I continue to grow my portfolio with more assets, and therefore can see patients if I choose. Much of my net wealth is tied up in my real estate business, which provides the passive income that is the foundation of my new freedom.

But that does not mean my work is done. I must now protect my assets.

ASSET PROTECTION

To maintain financial freedom, we must establish adequate asset protection. Yes, my story is about loving taxes and the benefits the U.S. tax code provides. That is one way of protecting assets.

Now we must discuss how to protect assets from the government that has provided the incentives to create wealth.

There are other threats, of course, such as financial pirates and other potential predators which include your business partners, employees, and tenants.

The method for protecting assets is guided by two goals:

Prevent a lawsuit.	Take away leverage.

PREVENTING LAWSUITS: FOLLOW THE MONEY

When you are considering an investment, it is wise to follow the money to learn who will benefit from your involvement. You? Your financial advisor?

When devising a play to protect your assets, you also want to follow the money so that you can learn who would benefit from a lawsuit against you. When making a list of who might sue, ask yourself who believes they can get their hands on your assets. People who believe they can get money from you may do everything in their power to use the court system to dip into your pocket.

And it is not just the plaintiffs that make money in a lawsuit. Lawyers make money, and sometimes more than the plaintiffs. It is often lawyers who convince their clients to file the lawsuit in the first place. That is why attorneys in the United States pay millions of dollars to run television ads throughout the day telling you to talk to them first if you have been involved in auto accident, for example, or otherwise feel damaged.

The key to protecting your assets from batch plaintiffs and their attorneys is to set up your business and investments so that if they do sue, they likely will not get any money.

Unlike many other countries, the United States allows lawyers to accept contingent fees. A contingent fee is paid only if the plaintiff wins the case or convinces you or your insurance company to settle the case. If you can convince the lawyers they will not get any money even if they win, then they likely will not take the case. Lawyers hate not getting paid.

How do you set up your business and investments so that the chances are slim that a plaintiff will get money from you even if they win a lawsuit? Full disclosure: I am not an attorney. However, my personal experiences, research, and working with an attorney have helped educate me. At the start, however, hire a qualified attorney to advise you and set up your own strategy.

THE RIGHT ENTITY

Just as protecting your money from the government requires the right entity structure, the most important step in protecting assets from plaintiffs is to use the proper entity for owning your business and investments. Remember that the laws that protect your assets from plaintiffs are often different than the tax laws. So, you want to form a tax strategy using entities that also protect you from future plaintiffs.

Make sure that your tax advisor has a good understanding of the asset protection rules in your state, province, and country as well as a thorough understanding of the tax law. You will also want your tax advisor and your asset protection attorney to speak to each other at least once or twice as you formulate your tax and asset protection strategy.

Fortunately, you can get both maximum tax savings and asset protection by using the right entities. There are many asset protection entities to consider.

TRUSTS

Trusts are particularly good for moving assets from one generation to another. They are also particularly good for asset protection.

Trusts have been available for thousands of years, so there are many cases telling us how trusts will be handled in a lawsuit. The general rule is that if the beneficiary of the trust is different than the grantor then creditors cannot get at the assets of the trust.

Let's say you want to leave your money to your children and that you want them to be taxed on the assets now but to not get the assets until after you die. You can do this by putting the assets into a trust. Another great aspect of trust is that the trust document says who can get the income as assets of the trust and when. The trust document, which you need to write with the help of an attorney, can specify when your children get the assets or income of the trust. In this way, you can control your assets even after you die.

You can also use trusts for giving assets to a charity. In fact, you can give the asset to the charity while keeping the income. This way, the charity gets the asset when you die. You get the income while you live, and the asset is protected from potential lawsuits. In addition, you can get a tax deduction for the charitable contribution now even though the asset isn't actually used by the charity until you die.

There are lots of uses for trusts in asset protection strategies. Once again, your attorney and tax advisor will help you create your own strategy for your situation.

PARTNERSHIPS

When it comes to asset protection, a partnership can be either very good or horrible.

General partnerships offer no protection from plaintiffs. You are liable for everything you do, everything your partner does, and everything your employees do. When someone sues a general partnership, they also sue all of the partners.

You don't have to have a written agreement to be considered a general partnership. So be careful.

Limited partnerships are good for asset protection because the limited partners do not have any liability for what goes on in the partnership. They can only lose their investment—no more. A limited partnership can be good for estate planning and for businesses where only one or two of the partners are running the business and the rest are passive investors.

CORPORATIONS

Corporations are good entities for protecting you from any lawsuits that are directed at the company. As a shareholder, you cannot personally be sued unless you personally did something wrong. You're a bit like a limited partner because all you can lose is the amount you have invested into the business. In countries other than the United States, where there aren't a lot of personal injury lawsuits, corporations can be great, so long as they also meet your tax goals.

LLCs

Limited Liability Companies (LLCs) can be the absolute best way to protect your business and investment assets from lawsuits. They give you the protection of a corporation. You can only lose what you put into the company. But they give you more protection than a corporation if you are personally sued. Limited Liability Companies generally have the protection of a charging order.

Here's an example of how a charging order works:
Our firm uses a lot of LLCs as asset protection. This way, if we have an issue with one of our properties, our investor partners and the principles are protected. A few years back we had a renter that lived in filth.

Despite numerous warnings after unit inspections, the tenants refused to keep the apartment tidy. For example, to reduce expenses, they chose not to use the air conditioner in the humid summer months. As a result, mold began to form. They were evicted after management received many complaints from neighbors concerned about their unkempt way of living.

Almost two years later, we received a certified letter informing us that the tenant filed a lawsuit, blaming us for the mold. They alleged that their child suffered respiratory issues which led to multiple ER visits for asthma exacerbations.

Initially, we were shocked since we had attempted numerous times to correct the issue. But we were not personally concerned about the lawsuit because the property was placed in an LLC, and we were properly insured. This is not unlike the physician that is suddenly in the crosshairs of a patient who files a complaint, yet clearly has an alternate sense of the reality of the situation. Such a lawsuit may be unfair, but that's why proper protection is essential.

Lawyers for plaintiffs understand LLCs, so they don't tend to sue people whose assets are protected this way. After all, lawyers like to get paid. Why take on a case that cannot win?

Be sure to have both an attorney and a CPA help you with your entity structure. The best way to do this is to begin with a good tax advisor. You and your tax advisor can devise a solid structure that will give you the best tax benefits. Then, go over this entity structure with your asset protection attorney. This order of due diligence will help you be efficient and effective.

Tax Concept/ Asset Protection
MIKE PINE

A good asset protection plan will also incorporate tax optimization strategies. Conversely, a bad asset protection plan may very well protect your assets from potential plaintiffs but could have severe, costly tax implications.

It is essential to have your tax planning partner work with your asset protection attorney when creating your plan and structure. Most asset protection attorneys are well versed in their area of specialty and are solely focused on liability protection, as they should be; however, this can sometimes inadvertently cause unanticipated tax consequences.

When an asset protection attorney works hand in hand with a tax CPA, they can meld the best of their respective two worlds to both protect everything you have worked hard to achieve while also reducing your current and future taxes.

chapter 13

Other Tax-Friendly Investments and Traps

My focus has been on commercial real estate investments. But I'm well aware of other investments that will enhance your tax pictures. Before I share those details, allow me to warn you about a popular investment vehicle that is inherently harmful if you are unaware of the tax hit.

Mutual funds are the most common form of stock market investing especially for busy doctors. The problem is that mutual funds contain a tax trap that many people don't know about.

Think of a mutual fund as a pass-through entity like a partnership. The income earned in a mutual fund is not taxed to the mutual fund. Instead, it is taxed to the investors. That might be okay if everyone entered a mutual fund at the same time. Everyone would simply report their share of gains and losses on the stocks sold in the mutual fund, and then they would see the value of their investment grow or decrease by those same gains and losses.

Unfortunately, that's not the way life works.

If you invest in mutual funds, you will likely buy into a fund that has been around for many years. Over the years, investors have come and gone while the fund has purchased many different stocks throughout those same years. The challenge comes when the fund goes to sell a particular stock. Let's say you decided to invest in Mutual Fund A at the beginning of the year. The fund bought company Stock B for $10 per share fifteen years ago. When you joined the fund at the beginning of the year, Stock B had a market value of $50 per share. The day after you join the fund, the fund managers decided to sell the stock. So there is a gain to the fund of $40 per share on the sale of Stock B.

Who pays the tax on the $40 gain? You do, even though you just joined the fund the day before. All investors who owned shares of Mutual Fund A on the day the mutual fund sold the stock share in the gain. Doesn't seem fair, does it? It gets worse.

Suppose you paid $100 per share for Mutual Fund A when you bought it in January. At the end of the year, the stock market takes a dip in value and now your shares of Mutual Fund A are only worth $80 per share. You still must pay tax on your share of the $40 gain from the sale of Stock B inside the mutual fund.

Mutual funds are one of the few places where you can lose money and still owe tax on your investment. Change your facts. Change your tax.

OIL AND GAS INVESTMENTS

The United States has long held an energy policy promoting oil and gas drilling operations inside the borders of the United States to help reduce dependence on foreign oil. The government has put this into action through the tax law by providing significant tax benefits for anyone who invests in domestic oil and gas drilling operations.

Oil and gas provide truly great tax advantages. Remember the discussion about passive income and passive losses earlier in the book? Oil and gas are the only investments that are not subject to these rules. That's right. If you invest correctly, you can deduct losses from oil and gas against ordinary income, even though your investment is entirely passive.

I first learned this when I was practicing medicine in East Texas. I was increasingly frustrated that there were many extremely wealthy people in my small town who had not sacrificed years of training and education to become a doctor or lawyer, and they were far better off financially than I was and rarely had to work. To my amazement, their annual taxable earnings, in many cases, were less than what I earned after spending massive hours in the emergency room. They were on perpetual vacation because they effectively paid no tax, or very little, thanks to their oil and gas investments. The reality did not just open my mind to changing the facts of my life. It blew my mind wide open and sent me in search of another way of generating income and tax efficiency.

FOUR OPPORTUNITIES

There are four types of investment in oil and gas. The first is to buy stock in an oil and gas company. This is treated like any other stock investment and has no special rules or benefits.

Second, you can buy an interest in the royalties from a producing oil and gas well. This income is portfolio income, and other than creating investment income so you can deduct investment interest expense, there are no great tax benefits from investing in a royalty interest.

The other two types of investments in oil and gas are both investments in the actual drilling operation— and they provide great tax benefits. *Exploration and Development.* Remember those terms.

Exploratory operations, also called "wildcat" drilling, can be very risky, as there is no assurance that there is oil in the ground where you are drilling. Also, this type of investment often has operational agreement clauses that can subject you to the requirement of adding more capital to your investment if the drilling wells are dry. Of course, with better and better technology, this risk is always decreasing with the better operators.

Development wells are drilled in established oil fields where the reserves of oil are proven. The developer may need more money to drill additional wells to get more oil out of the ground. This tends to be less risky than exploratory drilling, though you can still lose your money.

When a development company drills for oil and gas, it has two main categories of expense. The first is the equipment it purchases to drill. This is usually about 30 percent of the cost of drilling a well. The second is intangible drilling costs (IDC). IDC includes all of the other drilling expenses, including labor, survey work, ground clearing, drainage, fuel, and repairs.

These expenses normally would be a cost of the well and would be depreciated or amortized over the life of the well. Luckily, for oil and gas investors, our government decided to allow people to deduct both their IDC and their equipment costs in the year they spend the money, which is usually the first year of investment in the drilling operation. That means that 100 percent of your investment is typically allowed as a deduction in the year that you make your investment in the drilling operation.

Simple example: If you invest $100,000, you get a deduction for $100,000 the first year. At a 40 percent tax rate, that's equivalent to the government immediately giving you $40,000 ($100,000 × 40 percent = $40,000) for investing in the oil and gas operation.

This isn't the only tax benefit for investing in oil and gas. You also get to deduct 15 percent of the well's gross income each year. This is called depletion. It's like depreciation, only you get it every year, even after you have deducted all of the IDC and the equipment costs.

Depletion purposes includes all of the sales proceeds from the oil and gas, and it isn't reduced by any expenses. So, you could have $1,000 of gross income, and expenses of $400, for net income of $600. You would then get a depletion deduction of $150 ($1,000 × 15 percent = $150) and pay tax only on $450 of income. (That's $600 income, less $150 depletion.) Take this tax gift each year, even well after you have recovered all of your investment.

To qualify for IDC, equipment and depletion deductions, you must own a direct interest in the drilling operations. Owning stock in the drilling company or owning a royalty interest in the oil and gas doesn't qualify. Be sure to meet with your tax advisor about this before you invest in oil and gas.

One more tip: To get all the IDC and equipment deductions to which you are entitled, you must own your investment through a general partnership or sole proprietorship. You can't own it through a corporation, LLC, or limited partnership. If you live outside the United States, be sure to check on your country's tax laws to find out what tax benefits they allow.

MINING AND TAX BENEFITS

Mining operations have similar tax benefits to oil and gas development. You get depletion on the gross income from selling the minerals, and there is special treatment for the mining operation development expenses, much like IDC as well as deductions for equipment. Be sure to ask your tax advisor about which mining industries in your country get special tax benefits. One country may give tax benefits to coal, while others give special treatment to oil and gas, gypsum, or other minerals.

RENEWABLE ENERGY TAX BENEFITS

Renewable energy also enjoys special tax benefits in most countries, including energy, wind turbines, solar energy, and electric cars.

Governments love to encourage investment in new sources of energy. Tax benefits include investment tax credits for putting money in wind turbines (windmills), credits for buying solar panels, and credits for buying electric cars, or even for buying hybrid gas/electric cars. Some U.S. states also provide huge tax credits for investing in solar energy. And, so long as the equipment is used in business, 100 percent can be deducted in the year it is purchased.

PRECIOUS METAL TAX BENEFITS

Another commodity that has special tax breaks in some countries is precious metals, such as gold and silver. When you own gold and silver, you probably own it as insurance against inflation. So, you're going to own it for several years. When you sell your investment in gold and silver, the gain should be treated as a capital gain.

United States tax policy doesn't promote ownership of gold and silver. Instead, investment in precious metals is discouraged by providing a special, higher tax rate than other long-term capital gains tax rates.

At the writing of this book, the capital gains rate for gold and silver in the United States is 28 percent— almost double the rate for other capital gains. So, you may want to own your gold and silver inside your IRA or pension plan. Since you will own the metal for a long time and the tax is close to ordinary tax rates, you might as well postpone the tax through a government-qualified retirement plan. And if you own it through a Roth IRA, you will never pay tax on the increase in value of your gold and silver.

Tax Concept/
Passive Loss Rules

MIKE PINE

When you don't actively participate in a business, the income and losses from that business are treated as passive income and passive losses.

When you invest in oil and gas development, you probably won't actively participate. And in the first year, you'll quite likely share in a tax loss of 100 percent of your original investment. These losses will be passive and can only offset passive income, right? Wrong.

As of the writing of this book, there is an exception to the passive loss rules for oil and gas. Even though you don't actively participate in the business, losses from oil and gas are treated as ordinary losses, and you can take 100 percent of your losses against any kind of income.

But to be sure your losses are considered ordinary, you have to be very careful about how you own your oil and gas investment.
You have to own your interest in oil and gas development outright. You cannot own it through an LLC, LP (limited partnership unless you own a "General Partnership Interest"), or any other entity that limits your liability. Instead, you have to rely on the developer's insurance to protect you from any lawsuits or disasters. Usually, the developer will form a partnership for the investors, and everyone will be a general partner for the first year or two.

In the second or third year that you own the investment, when the well begins to produce taxable income, you can change your ownership to a limited partnership or LLC to protect you from future liability. Good oil and gas developers will automatically change your ownership from a general partner to a limited partner as soon as the investment begins earning income. So, your liability is only for the year or two that the developer is actually drilling the well.

chapter 14

Stress-Free Audits

When I first began investing, I was absolutely terrified of an audit. We have been programmed to think of an audit as a scary horrible ordeal where you are going to be put on a stand and cross-examined and forced to pay thousands of dollars. What could be worse than an audit?

The reality is, tax auditors are just normal people doing their job. Do you want to eliminate your fear of a tax audit? Be prepared.

But don't start the night before your meeting. There are steps you must take so that even the toughest auditor won't scare you. Of course, it is wise to reduce your chances of an audit by fully understanding the tax code. Yet, you cannot necessarily avoid audits throughout your investing life. So being prepared means deciding how you are going to handle the audit before it even comes.

YOUR TAX TEAM

The first and most important defense against a tax audit is to have a strong team in place. This begins with a tax advisor, who should also be your tax preparer. Your tax advisor is the person who should be on the front lines confronting the auditor. He or she will have been through the process many times and been successful. Your tax advisor should be the only person directly dealing with the auditor.

How your tax advisor works with your tax auditor will have a huge impact on the outcome of the audit. Therefore, choose someone who has excellent personal skills and treats all people with respect, especially government auditors. Division of labor is an important aspect of being prepared for an audit.

Next, hire an excellent bookkeeper or accountant. This person does not have to be your tax advisor/preparer. In fact, if your tax advisor is also doing your bookkeeping, then there is a good chance that you have a squirrel hunter on your team, not a big game hunter.

Your bookkeeper will keep track of all your records and documentation. In the event of an audit, you will be ready with accurate information. In most cases, a tax audit is going to focus on whether you reported all of your income and whether you took only those deductions that you were allowed under the law.

ACCOUNTING SOFTWARE

Accounting software is an important element because it accurately records all your income and expenses. There are many good programs available. Be sure you choose software that will give you both an income statement and a balance sheet. Some software only gives you an income statement. An income statement only shows your income and your expenses. The balance sheet is what helps you be sure that your numbers are accurate. Balance sheets show your assets (what you own), your liabilities (what you owe), and your equity (the difference between your assets and your liabilities).

If the government is auditing your business, one of the first things the auditor will ask for is your income statement and balance sheet. Having these readily available tells the auditor that you're serious about keeping good records.

RECEIPTS

The general rule is that you need receipts for any deduction you take on your return. Certain types of deductions require even more information than just a receipt. Deductions for meals and travel, for example, require a note on the receipt about who you were with, the business nature of your relationship, where you were, and what you discussed. I suggest you simply note that information on the receipt right when you get it.

There are a couple of different ways to store your receipts. Scanning the receipts into your computer is usually the easiest. There are good cell phone apps available for convenience. This method means you'll have the data at your fingertips if needed. And digital files don't take up space in your office.

If you want to keep the paper receipts, then just make file folders for each type of expense. Every time you spend money, you put the receipts in to the proper folder. Then when you go to prepare your tax returns, you know just where they are.

CORPORATE BOOKS

You should have a corporate book no matter what type of entity you own, even if it's not a corporation. The book organizes documents you need besides receipts and your bookkeeping records. Always keep contracts or other legal documents in a safe and secure place that's easily accessed. You should include a personal copy of your tax returns.

Tax auditors always ask for a corporate book. They're amazed when we actually give them one and it's in good order. Apparently, lots of business owners

don't keep their corporate books in goc
complete corporate book, tells the auditor that you care about your business and that your records are probably complete. The real benefit of this and the other good records is that the auditor will tend to believe your tax return and won't ask for much more support materials. It takes a lot less time to finish the audit, and because the auditor isn't looking as hard, they likely won't question much. That means that the auditor will not need to prolong the process.

Debbie F create complete corporate books? Jeff 23

Tax Concept/ Purchase an Audit Defense Plan
MIKE PINE

Since your tax preparer is the best person to meet with an auditor, it makes sense to also prepare an audit protection plan where available. This will likely include an extra fee that tends to be a percentage of the tax return preparation fee. It will cover the cost of the professional fees representing you in an audit. If you are audited, you should not have to pay for the time it takes to meet with an auditor and represent your business. However, without an already established audit protection plan, your tax advisor will not bill you for their time spent representing you.

The most expensive part of an IRS audit can be the professional fees you pay to defend your business. A typical audit can run $10,000 to $15,000 in professional fees. You may not pay any tax at all, and you still lose because of the cost of the professional fees.

An audit defense plan won't insure you against the taxes and interest you might owe, but it will protect you against most costs of defending yourself against the IRS. This is especially important because in an IRS audit, you are guilty until proven innocent. For this reason, it is wise to already be working with a top-notch tax advisor when possible. In that case, your audit defense plan will be a natural by-product of tax preparation services. Think of it as insurance. You hope you'll never have to use it, but should an audit happen, you'll be happy you planned ahead.

Don't forget the deduction. As explained in this book, any "ordinary and necessary" expense paid by a business is a tax deduction. Professional fees and items like audit protection plans are also deductible expenses.

chapter 15

Estate Planning Is Good Tax Planning

Estate planning comes down to two things: making it as easy as possible for your family to handle the financial aspects of your death, and making sure that all, or at least most, of your assets go to your family, your charities, and others you choose as beneficiaries—and not to the government.

Planning for my demise never seemed to matter much until my net worth hit a significant number. I was working a shift in the emergency room, taking care of an estate planning attorney of all things. We cordially struck up a conversation, and it was not long before my passion for tax and real estate spilled out, and he asked me a stunning question.

"What happens to all your assets when you die?"

I had spent so much time creating cash flow and a powerful financial machine that I had not considered the huge impact wealth could have on my family when, not if, I died. I was astonished by how easily the government and or legal processes could bring down all I had strived for. Needless to say, I engaged the services of that attorney, and we built a fortress to protect our family legacy from liability issues that might arise.

STEPS TO SUCCESSFUL ESTATE PLANNING

Let's review steps you should take to simplify the process your heirs will need to follow after your death. Our goal is to increase the amount of your wealth they get to keep. There are three *musts* on your to-do list:

1. Place assets in a trust.	2. Create a will.	3. Avoid estate tax.

STEP 1: PLACING ASSETS IN TRUSTS

As doctors, we understand mortality all too well. It is not enough to have life insurance so that there is enough money for your coffin and funeral expenses. More importantly, you must make sure that the ownership of your assets is automatically passed on to your family through a legal device before you die so that your family does not have to go through probate court.

Probate is the process of assessing an asset's title (i.e., who owns it) from the person who died to that person's heirs. Heirs are simply the people or organizations that get your assets when you die, such as your family or your favorite charity.

Avoiding probate is important because it can be expensive—i.e., lawyers will be involved, and you know how we doctors feel about lawyers. It is also a public procedure. Do you really want your family's financial information available for public review?

You remove probate from the equation by making sure each one of your assets is titled to a trust. You can be the trustee of the trust, and you can even be the beneficiary of the trust assets while you are alive.

The trust document states what will happen to your assets when you die. Basically, it sorts out who gets what so that your loved ones do not engage in emotional and difficult arguments and battles upon your death.

If charitable giving is important to you, then consider creating a charitable trust. This will allow you to donate to a charity while you are still alive and continue to receive the income stream of that asset until you die. This practice will also help you and the charity to avoid estate tax, not to mention provide you a charitable contribution deduction while you are still alive.

STEP 2: WHERE THERE IS A WILL

Just because you have created trust does not mean you can skip creating a rock-solid will, especially if you have small children. For one thing, a will allows you to appoint the person who will be the guardian of your children. In a will, you can also be very specific about who gets each asset, and you can detail your funeral requests and other special requests. Between a will and a trust, you should have most bases covered.

STEP 3: AVOIDING THE ESTATE TAX

If your estate is over the government's threshold of a specified amount when you die, that excess is assessed an estate tax. In 2021, the threshold is nearly $12 million for a single unmarried taxpayer. By 2025, the current administration in the White House is likely to roll it back to pre-2017 amounts of close to $5.5 million, or even less.

The IRS basically says that you can die with an estate up to the threshold amount, leave it to your heirs, and not pay tax upon your death. This has been the case for a long time. So, you might think that as long as you give away the money and assets before you die, you won't have a taxable estate upon your death. That's a loophole the IRS has tried to eliminate by taxing gifts.

Therefore, the estate tax threshold has been folded into a single item called the *unified gift/estate threshold.*

This means, anyone can either give, or beq
both, a combined total equal to the estate
taxable threshold during their lifetime.

For example, in 2021, while the threshold is set at
about $12 million for an individual, a person who learned
they had only a few months to live and would die
before December 31, 2021, could give away $6 million
and have another $6 million of their estate bequeathed
upon their death, before any gift or estate taxes would
be assessed.

The estate threshold essentially works like a unified
gift or estate tax credit by allowing any taxpayer to give
or bequeath the credit or threshold amount during their
lifetime before any tax is owed.

The trick is to try to *gift* away your estate in a way to
minimize the IRS's value of the gifts, so as to maximize
the value of the unified estate and gift credit.

One great way of doing this is using discounts
provided in Family Limited Partnerships (FLP). Two
such discounts are very common and are called
the marketability discount and the minority interest
discount.

An FLP is a great estate planning tool but must
be set up and continually maintained and advised by
competent tax and legal advisors—especially because
tax and estate laws are always changing. Speak to your
tax advisor for more details. But if that advisor is not
familiar with this important advantage, you may want to
seek advice elsewhere.

Tax Concept/ Marketability Discount/ Minority Interest Discount
MIKE PINE

A doctor has an estate worth $15 million, and the assets have been put into a Family Limited Partnership in return for 100 percent ownership of the FLP. The doctor has three married children and wants to give them 1 percent of the assets. The three heirs each receive 1/3rd (or 0.33 percent) of 1 percent in 2021 for a value of $50,000.

But since each child is only being gifted 0.33 percent of 1 percent, they are receiving a minimal interest of a large business that has no clear market to sell to. That would mean that even though on paper they have a $50,000 share of the partnership, they are unlikely able to sell it at full value, which creates the "marketability discount. For this reason, the IRS allows a marketability discount.

Most marketability discounts for minority interests are set at around 20 percent. So, an interest that is worth $50,000 in the partnership is discounted by the IRS so that only $40,000 is potentially considered a taxable gift.

A minority interest discount works this way: The FLP interest given to the doctor's three heirs are encumbered since they have very little say over how the FLP operates. The doctor controls the FLP in full, and regardless of what the children say, they can't force their parents to distribute any cash or assets to them.

In general, this minority interest discount is set again at around 20 percent. So even though the children and their spouses were gifted $50,000, their minority interest discount is worth 20 percent, which means if only considering the minority interest discount, their share drops to $40,000 in the eyes of the IRS.

However, the IRS allows a taxpayer to recognize both the marketability discount and the minority interest discount together.

This means any qualifying interest gifted to the children that is encumbered by both discounts of 20 percent is given a combined 40 discount. So, the $50,000 gift is in their pockets, but each heir's gift has a tax value of $30,000.

In 2021, this means the doctor has reduced the size of his estate by $150,000; yet, the IRS agrees that only $90,000 of the gift is taxable.

Now, remember, the gift tax and estate tax threshold is unified; and therefore, any taxable gifts (even if no tax is paid as they are part of the unified threshold) are combined with the value of the estate when you die. Currently, the IRS states that any individual can gift another individual up to $15,000 in a year without it impacting the unified threshold. So in the above scenario, both of the parents each gave their child a gift valued at $15,000 for a total of $30,000, and it doesn't count against the unified gift and estate threshold! This illustrates one more reason why it is important to always be planning regarding taxes and your money. If done smartly, Dr. Bliss can give away a substantial part of his estate of the years completely tax-free. and retain his entire gift and estate tax credit/threshold.

chapter 16
The Facts of Retirement

Retirement is not what it used to be. Literally. The most traditional idea of retirement originated in the late 19th century in Germany to provide pensions for the working class. The idea was that laborers reaching the age of 65 were required to cease working and enjoy the benefits provided to them by the state. This "must be present to win" policy worked out well for Germany since most workers had died long before reaching the mandated age.

Skip ahead. Eventually, the idea began to catch on and gradually spread westward in various forms, but eventually, people started living longer, making it harder to financially support the pensions. Enter the early stages of the traditional retirement plan where you invest and save until the age of 65, at which point you hang it up and start planning your cruise. Just one problem: people are not saving enough, and 65 isn't really the retirement age anymore.

Let's look at some the realities of today's retirement:

> **SAVINGS:** The average person waits too long to start saving. In addition, they begin their careers saddled with an average of $30,000 in student loans, leaving them even further behind. No wonder that according to recent surveys, the average 50-year-old has only $60,000 saved for retirement. In fact, less than 20 percent of people admit to being confident that they will even have enough to retire.

> **RETIREMENT AGE:** Sixty-five is no longer the magic number. More than half of all retirees retired earlier than they anticipated for reasons beyond their control, leaving them to either rethink their retirement strategy or end up as one of the nearly 20 percent of people 65 and older who are forced to work full- or part-time.

> **LIFE EXPECTANCY:** Long gone are the days of a 20-year retirement stash. One in four of today's 65-year-olds will live past 90, and one in 10

will live past 95. Now, factor in the additional years of the rise in cost of living. Increased life expectancy is great – if you can afford it.

HEALTHCARE: Living expenses are one thing but do not forget that to stay alive, you probably need healthcare. The average couple should expect to spend an additional $260,000 on this. If you are ambitious, plan on additional funds for assisted living and/or nursing home.

SOCIAL SECURITY: I am throwing this one in because I often hear people talking about it as though it will be the safety net. Not so fast. The average annual Social Security distribution in 2016 was $16,260 per year. That is great but hardly enough to live on.

Panicked? I get it. To be honest, I do not understand why we are still talking about and looking at retirement in the same way we did 50 or even as recently as 20 years ago. Everyone is living longer, but no one wants to work forever! Ye olde retirement is not going to cut it. I am not saying you shouldn't save for retirement. The problem is that often, by the time you start getting serious about retirement, it is too late. Or worse, you do everything right and still come up short. The traditional approach to retirement is a great foundation; it is just not enough.

Even as I joined the medical profession, I knew it was short-term and that I wanted to find another income stream to allow for flexibility in my long-term goals. Once I discovered the understanding of tax and investing, I was hooked. Medicine was changing, and I knew that ultimately it would not sustain the lifestyle that I wanted for myself and my family, particularly in retirement. I wanted the "golden years" to be just that: golden—or even better—platinum. Who wants to sit at home counting pennies when you finally have free time to enjoy?

In the years since I began changing my "financial facts of life," I have spoken with countless physicians about their long-term goals. Changes in the medical profession have drastically altered their income and, subsequently, their savings and retirement plans. Where once they pictured themselves retiring at a younger age and enjoying the fruits of their labor, they now envision postponing retirement to continue accruing savings. I have really enjoyed sharing with them the knowledge I have gained. In almost every instance, it was fear that has kept them from pursuing non-traditional paths of investing, to create a consistent, ongoing income stream. I cannot help but see this as a common factor among individuals weighing their options.

So, I will pose the same questions to you that I posed to myself: Why not make your money work for you instead of the other way around? Why not invest in yourself, in your education, in your business, so that when you want to retire you can retire?

You just must take the proverbial leap of faith, and then you will experience financial freedom, too. Just reading this book is proof that you are on your way to success.

THE CHALLENGE OF RETIREMENT

If you are aching to retire, I have some bad news for you. You have a challenge ahead of you—you may never be able to retire, at least not with the income you enjoy now while you are working. And this is especially true if you are using the same methods to retire that our parents used-relying on pension, profit-sharing, RRSPs, and 401(K) plans. These government-qualified retirement plans provide temporary tax benefits, but they are also the reason most people will never be able to stop working for money.

Here is how the basic government-qualified retirement plan works. You and/or your employer (as allowed or directed by the government) decide how much you put into the plan each year. Under a typical plan, you are not taxed on the income you put into the plan. This has the same effect as if you received the income and then received a deduction for putting it into the plan. In fact, some plans work just this way, as a standard IRA in the United States.

The money in your plan is then invested in some type of government-approved asset. Most governments require you to decide between mutual funds or an account that earns interest, called a guaranteed contract. If you have a self-managed or self-directed account, you have more options for your investment, and you have more control over where the money is invested.

Your money stays in the retirement account until you retire. At that point, you can take some or all of the money out. When you do take the money out, the government taxes you at ordinary income tax rates. The effect of this is to postpone or defer the tax on this income and the related earnings until you retire. The argument for this type of program is that this gives you a way to save for retirement without the added burden of paying taxes on the earnings of your retirement investment until you retire. When you retire, as the argument goes, you will be in a lower tax bracket because you will not need as much income, as your expenses will be lower.

There are some important exceptions to the general rule that government-qualified retirement plans postpone your tax. In a Roth IRA, you don't get a deduction when you put your money into the plan, and you don't pay tax when you or your employer puts money into your superannuation account. The account does not pay tax on the earnings, and you do not pay tax when you take the money out of the account.

Most tax planning in the United States, and around the rest of the world, is focused on maximizing the amount you can put into these types of accounts. The idea is that the more you put in the less you pay now and the more money you earn tax-deferred. If you are like most people, you've been told your entire working life to maximize your 401(k).

What I realized early on was that I never wanted to be ordinary, and I changed my facts. The conventional wisdom of retirement planning dictates that I will be in a lower tax bracket at retirement so that these funds I have deferred tax on will be taxed at a lower ordinary income bracket. This is great if you want to retire poor! If you plan on retiring with even the same amount of income you have while you are working, you will be in a higher tax bracket when you retire.

RETIREMENT = HIGHER TAX BRACKET

The reason for this is that while you are working, you can take advantage of a whole host of tax benefits. While you are working, you probably pay interest on a home mortgage. When you retire, you hopefully have paid off your mortgage, so you no longer have that deduction. While you are working, you likely have business deductions or employment-related deductions. These obviously go away when you retire.

There are people who say that the fact these deductions go away is precisely why you do not need as much income when you retire as you do while you are working. The point being that you don't have to pay for kids, a mortgage, and business expenses when retired. That may be true if you plan to just sit around the house and watch television when you retire. Not me: I intend to live my best life! As doctors, we have already delayed a tremendous portion of our lives in school, training, and early practice days so why would we want to change our status again? You just do not get all of the tax deductions you had while you were working.

This does not even take into account the effects of inflation on your tax bracket. You may be earning $100,000 now as a couple and be in a fairly low tax bracket. But by the time you retire, you may need $200,000 of income to maintain your current lifestyle. Tax brackets rarely keep pace with real inflation, so you could find yourself in a much higher tax bracket just from inflation.

This is not the only way you will end up paying more taxes by using government-qualified retirement plans. Typically, people will invest in the stock market.

What types of income do you earn from stock market investing? You earn capital gains and dividends.

When you invest in the stock market through a qualified retirement plan, like a 401(k), all the income you earn is eventually taxed at the regular tax rates. So, instead of the preferred capital gains rates, that same income is taxed from your retirement plan. *Here again, refer to the note on page 24 for additional information on capital gains rates.* This alone can more than double the tax rate on your investment earnings. The reality is that if you are going to have as much money when you retire as you do now, then you probably will be in a higher tax bracket than you are today.

In summary, you end up in a higher tax bracket with the same income. You shift 20 percent capital gains to 35 percent or higher ordinary income rates and inflation eats you into a higher tax bracket! *Remember this may change, as explained on page 24.* Wow. Those are staggering facts that I used to abide by—until I changed my facts of life.

Tax Concept/ Retirement

MIKE PINE

Dr. Bliss has a truly novel way of looking at retirement and planning for it. Conventional wisdom is simply that—*conventional.* Dr. Bliss has learned to implement extraordinary wisdom, and rather than produce conventional results, he continues to produce extraordinary results.

Tax law can also make an extraordinary impact on your retirement. As mentioned above, ROTH retirement accounts not only grow tax-free, but the distributions during retirement are tax-free. Contributions to ROTH accounts are not tax-deductible, though, so one must carefully balance their need for current tax deductions with their retirement planning strategy. A great tool that many tax professionals help their clients to utilize is surfing the tax brackets as part of their ROTH contributions, or better yet, ROTH "backdoor conversions."

As discussed elsewhere in this book, the concept of surfing tax brackets greatly impacts your current tax savings. This concept is very applicable to funding ROTH retirement accounts. Strategic planning of what your tax rates will be from one year to another can offer the opportunity to contribute to ROTH accounts in years when your income tax rates are at the lower end of the spectrum. In such years, you can choose to perform a "backdoor conversion," which allows you to convert a traditional retirement account into a ROTH account.

Utilizing such a maneuver helps you surf the tax brackets as a backdoor conversion and enables you to take deductions in the years you contribute to a standard retirement account. Then in a lower tax rate year, you can recognize the previous deductions as taxable income.

Basically, you are creating deductions in the years that you need them, then, in essence, returning those previously taken tax deductions in a year when you didn't need them—all the while increasing your ROTH retirement accounts.

Other great tax benefits that can help you plan for your retirement include utilizing the tax law to help set you up for the type of lifestyle that you want to have in retirement. By taking advantage of some select types of self-directed retirement accounts, you can acquire lifestyle types of assets that will be there for you when you are ready for them.

Take, for example, a physician that had a dream of owning a beach house for his retirement days. He had accumulated funds in a typical 401k that was invested in the mutual funds. With the advice of his CPA, he converted his 401k into a different type of retirement account that was used to purchase a large beach house while also leveraging debt at today's incredibly low-interest rates. He turned the beach house into an upscale vacation rental that is entirely self-funding its maintenance costs, including paying off the debt. He is also not paying taxes and his investment is growing in value as real estate prices continue to soar. In less than a decade, the physician will have his dream retirement home fully paid for and ready for him to move into the day he retires.

There are many tax-optimizing ways to enhance your retirement. Think outside the box, find a tax planning partner to help you make your retirement extraordinary, not conventional.

Made in the USA
Las Vegas, NV
31 March 2022

46619475R00111